CREATING CLOSER FAMILIES

CREATING CLOSER FAMILIES

PRINCIPLES OF POSITIVE FAMILY INTERACTION

William G. Dyer
Brigham Young University

Brigham Young University Press
Provo, Utah

Library of Congress Cataloging in Publication Data

Dyer, William G
  Creating closer families.

  Includes bibliographical references and index
  1. Family—United States. 2. Interpersonal re-
lations. I. Title.
HQ734.D984   362.8'2   75-20169
ISBN 0-8425-0729-9
ISBN 0-8425-0726-4 pbk.

Library of Congress Catalog Card Number: 75-20169
International Standard Book Number: 0-8425-0729-9 (cloth)
                                    0-8425-0726-4 (paper)
Brigham Young University Press, Provo, Utah 84602
© 1972, 1975 by Brigham Young University Press. All rights reserved
Third printing 1980
Printed in the United States of America
80   1.5Mp   45679

CONTENTS

PREFACE

This book is written about and for families. Underlying everything is the hope that it will encourage family members to revive those feelings all of us have had that "we really ought to make some changes" and to actually begin to take some needed action. A wise man has truly said, "No success can compensate for failure in the home." Almost all who are still connected with their families will *say* that improving their relationships with family members is a high-priority item, but some limitation may keep them from taking action consistent with these values. Sometimes it is a lack of skill — not knowing exactly what to do. More often the hesitancy stems from feelings of anxiety and fear — fear that if they try something different a most important person (like a spouse or son or daughter or parent) will in some way reject an offering to change.

Hopefully something in this volume will stimulate someone in the family to say to others, "I'm concerned about how we are functioning as a family. I care about us. I would like to talk about how I feel and let you know what I would like to see happen in our relationships."

The beginning of change is caring enough about others to begin to share our feelings and concerns. If there is enough caring and sharing then it is possible that a new style of family life can emerge — a life filled with love and trust. Trust is a central dimension in the closer, more effective family. There are many families who deeply love each other but cannot trust each other — to express that love in word and action, to keep commitments, to live up to priorities, to be constant and consistent in caring, to be available in time of need, to be sensitive, to forgive, to help, and finally to honestly give of oneself. One goal of any family change

vii

is to achieve higher trust, for that is the basis of most subsequent positive interaction.

There is no particular order in reading the sections in this book. One may read any chapter independently of the others. Some chapters are written more for parents, some for husbands and wives, some for children, and some for the whole family. Perhaps if children could read about parents they might understand their own father and mother better, be more responsive and supportive, and prepare more carefully to guide the lives of their own children. Parents may be able to see in these pages something in the world of their children that they have missed or forgotten. It is sometimes hard for a father to recall when he was six or twelve or eighteen. He sees the world through forty-year-old eyes when trying to understand the world of his teenager. Concurrently, the teenager may be so locked into his own situation that he may not realize the needs of his parents — they need love and understanding too. But if all family members would call time out and talk and share and feel together, and then plan and build a set of actions that would represent something better than they have had before, perhaps greater joy and growth will follow.

There are many who have contributed to the creation of this volume. The family in which I was reared fashioned the original view of the problems and prospects of family life. As imperfect as it was, there was established a core of love and concern that is still a base of family interaction. My own wife, Bonnie, and our children — Gibb, Mike, Lisa, Jeff, and David — have been the center of my own life. No success I will ever have will compensate for a failure to achieve the love, trust, and growth I desire for all of us. Some may wonder if the writer of such a book as this is capable of practicing what he preaches. No one is as good as he would like — we all fall short of our own ideals — and so it is with me. But I have tried and am happy with the results.

The writings and teachings of Jack R. Gibb have been an important influence in my thinking, as have the life and influence of Reed Bradford of Brigham Young University, one of my early teachers, my colleague and friend, whose teachings and example have been a pattern for me to follow.

I wish to acknowledge the continual assistance of Gail W. Bell of Brigham Young University Press, the work of Elizabeth Thorpe, the editorial consultant on the book, for her gentle directions toward completion, and the skillful editing of Cynthia Gardner.

CREATING CLOSER FAMILIES

1

CHANGE
THE PATTERN

The relationship between two people is a complexity of subtle connections and intertwinings. Through the years a man and his wife build a complementary set of expectations and reactions that sometimes persist despite all attempts to change. Often at first there is a conscious desire to please each other, but as the years go by a different pattern becomes defined and emerges in various designs that reflect habitual and unconscious responses to each other. People often do not intend to build the kind of relationship they ultimately develop, but as time passes the pattern solidifies. Many couples suddenly come to the realization that each is really not happy or satisfied or fulfilled in the marriage. They are not exactly sure why not, but something is amiss.

That patterns develop from simple things is illustrated in this story:

> At first Tom feels resentful when his wife, Laura, begins to turn over quietly and slip off to sleep instead of kissing him warmly and responsively and saying "Goodnight." Tom feels somehow rejected, less masculine and dominant. His fantasies include such conditions as another man in Laura's life, his own loss of attractiveness, the possibility of Laura's being frigid. Whatever the cause, he knows he feels diminished in some way. His wounded ego will not let him ask his wife the reasons why.

If he could ask, and if Laura could verbalize her feelings, Tom would learn that two pregnancies and the harrying pressure of a son, age three, and a daughter, age one, leave Laura more interested in sleep than in anything else. Fear of another pregnancy depresses her responsiveness, and Tom's hurt and yet demanding reactions leave her wanting to escape into sleep.

So a pattern develops. Tom's response is to behave in kind. He turns his back and goes quickly to sleep, and almost without their knowing it five years go by. In that time Tom and Laura lose the satisfaction of their warm relationship. They come to accept the condition as the "way things are" between them.

Neither Tom nor Laura likes the patterns they are in, but they don't quite know how to break out. For each, it would mean taking the risk of possible rejection. Tom would have to admit he wants more responsiveness than Laura is capable of giving at this time. And what if she confirms his fantasies that she really finds him personally unattractive?

Rather than risk the possible confirmation of his negative fantasies, Tom remains silent, and an important groove (or rut) in the interpersonal pattern develops. On the other hand, Laura, who is at first relieved with Tom's accommodation, later becomes distressed but isn't quite sure what will happen if she alters the prevailing condition. She has her own fantasies about what might happen if she initiates warmth again: Tom might reject her this time, or he might become increasingly demanding. She concludes it is better to let sleeping dogs lie. And she feels a little guilty as the old adage slips across her mind.

Thus many similar patterns become set. For example:

1. John gets so used to his wife's telling him what to do that he quits listening. His wife continues her barrage of nagging in the vain hope that it might make a difference.

2. Phil enjoys a regular set of activities with his old buddies — fishing, golf, and bowling. His wife resents it and constantly looks for faults in his friends. Her comments increase Phil's stubbornness and determination to

continue with "the boys."

3. Marian doesn't enjoy housework, and her home is often left untidy. Jim doesn't like the mess, but he feels that if that is how she wants it he will throw his things around too and increase the general disarray.

Each person in a marriage partnership has expectations the other doesn't understand. When these expectations are violated, a common response is some type of negative reaction. Then both partners begin to accept the less desirable condition as "the way it is." But there are very few things that have to stay the way they are.

To change a pattern often does not demand a major, disruptive, climactic alteration, but even a small variation will lead to a changed response. As in the old law of physics, any action leads to an equal reaction, and sometimes the reaction is more than equal in a positive direction.

If Tom could begin to caress his wife's cheek, tell her he loves her, and then turn over to sleep, there is a good chance it would in time lead to at least an equal reaction. If Laura could do something similar, express her fears and fantasies, or tell him about the ideal state she would prefer, perhaps a change would occur.

There is a tendency for each to place the blame for the pattern on the other, and the starting of a pattern may indeed be the fault of one of them. But the final pattern in a relationship is woven by both, and the change can be initiated by either. To change, at least one of them must say either to himself or aloud to the other, "I don't like the way it is. I want it to be different."

Following that declaration, one must do something that breaks the pattern — begin to listen, stop watching TV, begin to talk about the day's work, hold a chair for the other at the table, pick up the pajamas, or give a goodbye or welcome-home kiss.

Negative fantasies can be wrong.

2

ADJUST EXPECTATIONS

Marital Expectations

Every person comes into marriage with a set of expectations — about himself and about the new marriage partner. The new husband expects that he will behave in certain ways (self-expectations): he will make the living, take care of the car, help sometimes with the housework, go fishing and hunting with the "boys," and become the father of three sons. He also expects his wife to do certain things (expectations of others): she will always look pretty and trim, keep up the house, pay the bills, always be responsive and affectionate, and be the mother of three sons.

The new wife also has a wide range of self-expectations: she will work for the first two years, do her share of the housework, cook, have a wonderful outdoor life with her husband, go to lunch with her girl friends, be active in church, visit her family regularly, and become the mother of two girls. Also, she expects her husband will help her cheerfully with the housework, take her with him on his outdoor trips, make the living, work in the church, and be a good father to their two girls.

Both have been building their vast expectation systems all through the years from watching their own parents and other adults, from things they have read, ob-

7

served, or imagined. They have expectations about everything — food, TV, money, visiting, love, friends, children,
holidays, and on and on. Expectations are so pervasive
that most people are not aware of them and how strongly
they influence everyone's behavior and reactions to other
people. If her expectations of him agree with his expectations of himself, subsequent interactions will dovetail,
their behavior will be complementary, and the end result
will be each rewarding the other with smiles, praise, and
good feelings. On the other hand, if what she expects of
him does not agree with what he expects of himself,
subsequent interactions will be variant and discordant
and will result in disappointment, upset, irritation, criticism, and/or withdrawal. The same is true about his
expectations of her.

Unfortunately, most young people spend very little
time trying to understand their own expectations or the
expectations of their future marriage partner. It becomes
a whole new world to try to comprehend when married
life begins. Ninety percent of all married couples will admit they have to work out adjustments in their expectations. (The other ten percent are probably lying.) Adjustment means change. Somebody has to change something — either an expectation about self, or an expectation about the other. For a marriage to bring enough
satisfaction to allow it to mature and develop, there must
be enough matching expectations in the critical areas of
interaction to allow positive rewards to be exchanged and
appreciated. Relationships deteriorate if there are too
many mismatched expectations, too many disappoint-
ments, too much discord.

Here is an example of marital problems caused by mismatched expectations:

> Bob has just left the apartment for his first day of work
> after the honeymoon. June is delighted to be alone in her
> first home. She plans her day. First she will get everything
> shining clean, then she will shop and prepare dinner. In
> her mind's eye, she can see the events of the evening.
> Everything will be lovely — dinner ready, candlelight, and

8

soft music, she will be dressed in her blue dress, and then Bob will come home. She tingles in anticipation. He will kiss her tenderly, tell her how wonderful everything looks, they will hold hands as they eat, and he will touch her face. After dinner they will do the dishes together and then cuddle together on the big sofa. Oh, she can hardly wait!

Bob finally arrives. He has been waiting to get home, too. He wants to be in his own home at last where he can kick off his shoes, have dinner ready, prepared by his wonderful little wife, and then watch TV. He is tired and hungry, and as he comes into the apartment, the smell is great. Giving his wife a quick kiss, he says, "What smells so good? I'm starving."

June can't believe it. He doesn't notice how clean everything is, the dress, the candlelight. "Meatballs," she says, "we're having meatballs."

"That's great!" Bob exclaims. "I love meatballs."

Shortly he is at the table shoveling in the meatballs when suddenly something clicks in his awareness. He feels that something is wrong. June is awfully quiet and is just picking at her food. "Anything the matter?" he asks.

"Oh, no," she answers in a quivering voice, "everything is just fine."

Now he knows something is wrong. He puts down his fork and with concern says, "What's the matter, June? Have I done something wrong?"

June jumps from the table and says, "Oh, you wouldn't understand," runs to the bedroom, throws herself on the bed, and begins to cry.

She is right — Bob doesn't understand, but he pleads at the bedroom door. "Don't cry, June, I can't stand that. Whatever I've done, I'll never do it again."

Lying on the bed, June begins to think. "It's really kind of silly to expect him to be so observant and attentive. After all, he does have some good qualities. He's clean and hard working." With that she dries her eyes and comes out to her husband.

Again he asks, "What's the matter?"

"It's nothing," she lies. "I'm just overly excited."

Although they kiss and make up, the fundamental mismatch between expectations is still unexplored. They did repair the emotional breach between them, which is a critical step in adjustment, but the probability of another disappointment for June — more tears and resentment —

is still lying in wait.

There are some hopeful signs for Bob and June. Bob is aware that something is not altogether right when he comes home and concentrates on meatballs. June is also beginning to learn that Bob is not everything she fancied. She may be able to change some of her expectations of what he will do and continue to appreciate his good qualities and what he does do. But they still have not learned to share their expectations with each other, for with insight it is possible that Bob could learn greater attentiveness and consideration, and this change in his behavior would please June as it met her expectations.

Sometimes an argument can bring mismatched expectations into the open, as in the following story:

> When Jerry leaves for his first day of work, he fully expects to return to an immaculate apartment, dinner ready, and everything prepared for his triumphal return. That's the way it always was when his father came home — everything in order and everyone waiting to serve the master of the house. He doesn't really understand that Ann comes from a drastically different household where there were no set routines, where nothing was planned or scheduled. Picnics were spontaneously assembled, or the family might suddenly decide to roast wieners in the fireplace or run out to a drive-in. It was a big, bustling beehive of a family.
>
> Thus Jerry is totally unprepared for the scene that meets his horrified gaze when he walks through the front door. The morning paper is scattered around the front room, the bed still unmade, silk stockings drying over the shower rod in the bathroom, and dishes still in the sink. Ann? She has been helping a girl friend make a new dress all day and has returned just a few minutes before Jerry. She feels hungry and is in the kitchen whipping up a batch of fudge.
>
> Jerry, with his violated expectations, wanders into the kitchen. "When did it hit?" he asks sarcastically.
>
> "When did what hit?" responds Ann with surprise.
>
> "The tornado. It really scattered this place around."
>
> This is not how husbands are supposed to behave. Husbands are supposed to come in, see the fudge, and say, "Oh, goody! Fudge. Let's fix some popcorn and have a party." Responding now out of her unmet expectations, Ann says,

"If you think I'm going to spend the whole day keeping house, you need to think again."

"I don't expect you to spend the whole day. Only fifteen minutes. Just pick up the big pieces."

"If you think I'm going to be like your mother — "

"You keep my mother out of this."

And Jerry and Ann are in the middle of their first real fight, and it certainly will not be their last unless they can work out some form of adjustment.

Unlike Bob and June, this couple has the issue right out in the open, and in some respects the adjustment can be handled more easily. At least the adjustment possibilities are fairly apparent:

Adjustment possibility 1. If Jerry says, "Ann, I can't live in a disorderly home. In order for me to be happy, you will have to keep things in place," Ann must be prepared to accept this and change her old style to meet Jerry's expectations.

Adjustment possibility 2. If Ann says, "I cannot be happy in a scheduled, orderly world like your family's. I must have more freedom and find happiness in our relationship and not in routines," Jerry will need to understand this and change his expectations and fit into a new life style.

Adjustment possibility 3. Jerry may say, "Ann, I won't expect you to clean house like my mother, but will you at least keep things picked up and have the bed made? I can't stand an unmade bed."

Ann will need to respond, "All right, I'll try to be more orderly if you won't compare me to your mother and if you'll try to relax a little and surprise me with a change once in a while."

In the first two possibilities either one or the other would make a change. Possibility 3 would require both to change somewhat. In each case there would need to be a change in somebody's expectations and attendant behavior, so there would be a matching of mutual expectations resulting in rewards for both. They would also need to repair any emotional breach (kiss and make up), so they feel good toward each other.

People can live together for years and never really understand the expectations that they violate regularly. They can live in a constant state of frustration and dissatisfaction. Couples who cope successfully with adjustments to mismatched expectations develop ways to share their expectations either openly or subtly and find either the insight or the flexibility to make some alterations either in the expectations of the other or in their own behavior.

A common reaction to unmet expectations is to "sweat it out." The person with the unmet expectations determines he will not say anything but will just keep quiet, suffer like a good soldier, and hope that in time things will get better. Research evidence shows that he really does not hide his disappointment totally from his spouse, who knows something is wrong but is not sure exactly what it is. There results a kind of game in which one tries to find out what is wrong and the other tries to keep him from doing so. Research also indicates that husbands more than wives try to use the keep-quiet-and-sweat-it-out method. More often wives will try to talk about differences or will get upset and make a scene over the problems. Adjustment can be facilitated if the unmet expectations can be brought out in the open so the possible alterations in expectations or behavior can at least be considered.

One young couple, married for a year, suddenly dissolved the marriage. The wife went back to her family home and obtained a divorce. When friends asked the husband what had happened, he said, "I don't know. There was something wrong, but she would never talk about it. She always said it was something she would have to work out herself."

The young husband was caught in an impossible situation. Obviously something needed to change, but without having any information, he did not know what he could do or what needed to be done to help his wife resolve her disturbances or dilemmas.

Expectations and the Total Family

Thus far this discussion has dealt only with expectations between husband and wife. Obviously the same message could apply to any situation involving anyone in the family. Parents often have expectations about how children ought to behave, study, treat their elders, handle their money, do work around the house. Children sometimes find they are getting the silent treatment or the hurt look from mother or dad, and they are not sure exactly what they have done. If they find out, they don't understand because to them their offense was "no big deal," but it may have violated a sensitive expectation of the parent.

Children also have expectations of parents that parents may never really understand. Children may like parents to be seen but not heard when their friends are around, to look appropriate in public, not to make a scene when the restaurant bill is added wrong, not to get uptight if an exam is flunked once, to try to understand rather than jump to conclusions.

It is not uncommon for children to feel frustrated and powerless when parents violate their expectations, for they feel their parents are too powerful in the parental driver's seat for them to handle. Children may then adopt a sweat-it-out stance, waiting for the time when they can leave home, and sometimes the parents are secretly relieved when the children go. There has been too long a pattern of undiscussed and unresolved strain and conflict.

Resolution of differences of expectations can be achieved. It takes talking, time, tenderness, and sometimes toughness. When a difference in expectations occurs, one person would like the other to change so that the first could keep himself intact. However, each person has direct control over himself (usually), and the first line of change may be to see how he could alter his own behavior or expectations to meet the expectations of others. If one is willing to make some change, the other may also take heart and find the resources to enter into an adjustment.

13

3

BE AUTHENTIC

Have you ever found yourself in the following kinds of situations?

1. At a party a person tells an antiblack story. You resent the story but do not say anything — and then feel somewhat ashamed of your own cowardice.

2. You hear a moving talk at a church, civic, or club meeting. After the meeting you want to express your feelings to the speaker, but shyness or something keeps you quiet.

3. There is a moment when you look at your mother, father, spouse, or friend, and a wave of deep love and appreciation sweeps over you, but for some reason you say nothing — and the moment passes.

4. In a meeting two people engage in a quarrel not related to the agenda of the meeting, and a great deal of time is wasted. Later the chairman asks how the members felt about the meeting and whether anything could be done to improve future meetings. You sit silent.

If you identify with any of the above situations, you are fairly normal. Most of us find it difficult to express our true feelings, especially when we are not sure how people will respond. Currently there is a movement on the part of applied behavioral scientists to reexamine and encourage the building of "authentic" relations, those relationships between friends, family, church members, and

15

co-workers where people have enough deep concern for each other that they do not always try to hide their true feelings from each other. It is difficult to know exactly how to represent our true selves in particular situations, especially when sensitive areas are involved. Consider the following incidents:

Jeff Hudson is back on campus for his second year. His most recent roommate, Dick Harmon, is a tall, friendly, hard-working young man from a small rural town. It is during the hot, steamy Indian summer that they begin their year's relationship. After a busy day in class the two roommates return to their quarters. Harmon wearily kicks off his shoes, peels off his socks, and with obvious relief begins to systematically clean out the accumulation of dirt and grime between his toes with his forefinger. Jeff watches with a kind of horrified fascination, but he cannot bring himself to say anything.

Thereafter Jeff watches this daily ritual with increasing disgust. He begins to gripe at Dick constantly, and their relationship disintegrates badly. Dick Harmon is dismayed, for he feels something is wrong, but he can't understand what he may be doing to upset his roommate.

Finally, Jeff has reached his limit. One evening as he watches the finger go through Dick's toes, he blurts out harshly, "Dick, I can't stand to watch you do that disgusting thing of cleaning between your toes."

Harmon looks up and quietly says, "I'm sorry, Jeff. I didn't know it bothered you. Why didn't you tell me?"

The Dixons are having a husband-and-wife chat. Mrs. Dixon is confiding in her husband that she is about at her limit in her relationship with their neighbor, an energetic widow, Mrs. Wilson.

"The problem," says Mrs. Dixon, "is that whenever we get together, Thelma Wilson always dominates the conversation, and the essence of every visit is to listen to her complain about how bad everything is. She is always upset over something or somebody. I sit and listen to her complain about the city government, the poor postal service, the neighbor's dog, the unfriendly neighbor on the other side of her, the ill-mannered Peterson kids, and on and on. I get so exasperated with her I don't know what to do."

Mr. Dixon listens quietly. He knows, as his wife does, that Thelma Wilson is also a very good neighbor in many ways. She is generous and willing to help others in need, an active church member. He asks his wife, "What do the other women in the neighborhood do about Thelma?"

"We've talked about it," says Mrs. Dixon, "and most of the other girls have handled it by avoiding her as much as possible. They don't feel very good about that, but what else can they do?"

Why didn't Jeff speak out earlier? Why don't the neighbors share their feelings with Thelma Wilson? It isn't easy to tell someone about our feelings concerning their personal habits or behaviors. We are afraid we might offend them or hurt their feelings or they might get angry and attack us, so we keep quiet. Commonly, we may also try to avoid the person, and as a result a break occurs in the relationship.

When to Reveal Feelings

Should we speak out whenever anything a person does bothers us? Obviously not, for if a person's behavior bothers us, it is *our* problem. We first need to see if we can expand our margin of tolerance and acceptance so we can accept that person for what he is rather than demand that he change so we feel better. However, if the person's behavior violates an important value of ours, or if we find for some reason we cannot expand our margin of acceptance adequately, then we should go to him and talk with him about our feelings of concern. The spirit of the encounter should be one of wanting to improve our relationship, based on a genuine concern for the other person.

Some people find it difficult to let others know when they are hurt, angry, upset, or even when they disagree. They keep their feelings hidden so that they neither resolve them by means of self-understanding and self-dialogue nor discuss them with others in a way that will be helpful rather than hurtful. Still others find it difficult to share their feelings of love, concern, joy, empathy, or appreciation. They keep these feelings locked inside

17

themselves where none can bask in the glow of the shared warmth. Positive feelings need not always be openly expressed, but neither should they always be hidden. The following experience shows the happiness that can come from expressed feelings of love:

> On the day before Christmas Mr. Brown drives into his driveway after a long day's work. He notices with interest that the driveway and walks that were covered with ice and snow when he left for work are now completely cleared. To himself he muses, "I wonder who Mother got to do that job."
>
> He goes into the house and takes off his coat and gloves. In the kitchen he meets his oldest boy, a lanky youth of thirteen. "Dad, did you notice the walks were all cleared off?" asked the boy.
>
> "Of course, I couldn't miss that."
>
> The boy then continues, "I didn't have any money to buy you a Christmas present so I cleaned the walks to show you that I love you and appreciate you." And then to the father's deep delight and surprise, his son walks over, puts his arms around his father, and hugs him tightly in an awkward embrace. The father hugs back, grateful for a gift he will never forget.

Why are we afraid, embarrassed, or reluctant to share our warm and positive feelings with others? The resistance usually comes from what we *imagine* might happen: the others might be embarrassed; they might suspect our motives; they might cry and that would put us in a situation that would be uncomfortable. We might appear awkward, or we might even cry — and that would be even worse. Sometimes we are stopped because we feel there is not enough time, or too many people are around. The person who fears an authentic encounter with another can find many reasons why he should stay behind his mask and not let anyone know his true feelings.

Shakespeare felt that being authentic was the beginning of moral behavior: "To thine own self be true, And it must follow, as the night the day, Thou canst not then be false to any man." To be false to yourself is to not let your behavior represent what you really are like inside.

One man put it this way: I am tired of having two opposing sets of feelings. When I have pretended to be good and people praise me, I often feel guilty and think, "If they really knew me they probably wouldn't like me." On the other hand, when I have done something inadequately or ineptly and people respond negatively, I think, "If they really knew me, they would like me."

This man decided that the best solution was to try as best he could, all the time, to let his behavior represent what he was truly like inside. Then, if people liked that, they would really like him, for that would be the kind of person he honestly was; and if they didn't like that behavior, he'd know they didn't like him, for he would represent his values as best he could.

Taking a Risk

Sometimes there are things about ourselves we don't like and would like to change. If we want to be authentic, we have to admit our weakness to others and honestly try to engage in actions that will help us eliminate or change our behavior. A person with a sharp tongue that wounds others' feelings should not say, "That's the way I am. And if I am to be authentic, I will just have to tongue-lash people and hurt them." If that person has other values, such as wanting to be kind and responsive to others, to build people rather than diminish them, he must be honest to those values too. This honesty would lead him to try to eliminate his sharpness of tongue.

Being an authentic person is a risk. Most of us have hidden behind a facade in some areas for so long that it would be a real risk to try to be different. It would be a risk for a teenage girl to go to a boy who is a fine example in the high school and say, "Greg, I want you to know I admire you and appreciate the good example you have set for me and the other kids in school." It would be a risk for a man to go to his boss and say, "I have been complaining about some things in the company to my family and others, and I think you should know how I feel. I

19

would like to meet with you and tell you my reactions in a way that I hope might help make this a better place to work." It is a risk for a father who has been silent too many years to tell his twenty-year-old son, "I love you, son. You are the most important thing in the world to me." Similarly, it would be a risk for the son to share such feelings with his father.

It may be true that nothing is gained or learned without a price. Behavior change has its price — anxiety and the possibility of failure. It is also possible that a change in the direction of being more authentic may have rewards that far exceed the costs.

4

COMMUNICATE*

Warning: Communication is a means to an end — not an end in itself. We can use communications to hurt, punish, and offend or to bind together and increase love and joy. The great skill sometimes is *not* to get people to communicate more, but to get them to communicate wisely and effectively. Too many families already communicate too many of the wrong things, and to encourage them to communicate more would only compound the disaster. Other families suffer from communication shortage; too many things remain unsaid and are not discussed.

Unintended Communications

Very simply, communication is the process whereby one person, through the use of symbols (words, actions, gestures), makes others understand how he thinks and feels. Sometimes we send out signals, unintentionally, that let people know how we feel when we might have preferred to keep our feelings hidden.

One problem in most families is that in certain areas the communication system is too good; that is, more is communicated than is really intended. We marvel at the sensitivity of the gleaming fingers of a radio antenna and their ability to pluck sound waves from the air. But mar-

*Revised. Reprinted by permission from the *Improvement Era*, "Improving family communications," April 1963.

velous, too, is the sensitivity of a little child, whose receptors are able to pick up all kinds of messages. One study of very young babies found that, if a baby were fed orange juice by a nurse who did not like orange juice, in a short time the baby would not like it either. However, if the nurse liked orange juice, so did the baby. Somehow, the nurse was able to communicate to the child her distaste for orange juice via tenseness, grimacing, or shuddering at the sight of the baby drinking the "nasty stuff."

If a baby is sensitive enough to pick up from his nurse how she feels about orange juice through her subtle body actions, what messages do children receive from parents in incidents like the following?

> Father talking to mother in the car on the way home from a parent-youth meeting: "What a boring meeting that was! I don't know the last time we had a really good speaker. I'd have gained more from staying home and reading a good book."
>
> A week later, the same father says to his son, "What! You don't want to go to the parent-youth meeting? I can't understand that. You never see me staying home from those meetings! I think they are important for good family relationships!"

One might guess that the father, unintentionally, has really communicated to his son his true feelings about such meetings: namely, that the good meeting (not found very often) is one where there is a speaker who is interesting and entertaining (to father).

Another interpretation may be that the father has both positive and negative feelings about going to parent-youth meetings. He may enjoy the topic and the general discussion but dislike the speaker. However, his pattern of communication, developed over a long period of time, is to talk only about things he dislikes. Thus his son is unaware of his other feelings. The result is unbalanced communication — the father has communicated too much about his negative feelings and too little about his positive feelings.

Here is another example of unintended communication:

Father talking to daughter: "I think you ought to read more of the good magazines we get each week instead of the trashy fan magazines you read all the time. After all, we spend quite a bit on the good publications."

In his daughter's hearing, the next day he says, "Any mail today? Oh, just the news magazine! We haven't had any important mail for a long time."

Children pick up all the communicative signals their parents give — not just what is spoken directly to them. In the above illustration, the father's intentions in his direct communication with his daughter are to encourage her to read good publications more, but his unintended communication tells her that he really thinks such magazines are not very important as compared with other matters. He is also saying that he is concerned more about wasting money than he is about the reading.

Or what about the following exchange?

Son (to father): "Dad, will you come and help me fix my wagon?"

Father: "Just a minute, son, I'm busy right now reading the paper."

Father (later): "Son, come and eat. It's time for dinner."

Son: "Just a minute, Dad. I'm fixing my wagon."

Father: "Not in 'just a minute.' When I call you I want you to come right now."

What is the father unintentionally communicating to his son? The son perhaps "hears" that there are two standards — one for him and another for his father. Or he hears that his father's newspaper is more important than helping him with his problems. If we were to ask the father, "What is more important, your newspaper or your son's problems?" he would undoubtedly insist that his son is more important. But in a number of subtle ways he has communicated to his son that the newspaper, or the television program, or the golf game really comes first in actual practice.

"Dad, will you
come and help me
fix my wagon?"

"Just a minute, son,
I'm busy right now
reading the paper."

The above cases indicate that unintentionally we communicate to other people our likes, dislikes, preferences, and disgusts. It would appear that at least one important basis of "good" communication is not to learn how to say the words better, but to examine ourselves and begin to alter those attitudes, feelings, and reactions that we would not like to see fostered in our children.

Blocked Communications

One of the strange paradoxes in human interaction is that at the same time people are unintentionally communicating things about themselves to others, they are also being very careful to avoid, hide, camouflage, or ignore other things about themselves and others, and in such areas there is little communication — intentional or unintentional. Consider the following example:

> Marriage counselor: "Mrs. Gray, what seems to be the biggest problem you have with your husband?"
> Mrs. Gray: "Ever since we were married, my husband has been thoughtless and neglectful. He no longer praises me or tells me he loves me. He forgets birthdays and anniversaries. He doesn't perform the courtesies and niceties that I would enjoy so much."
> Counselor: "Have you ever told your husband how you feel?"
> Mrs. Gray: "I should say not. If he isn't understanding enough to sense how I feel, I'm certainly not going to say anything. Besides, if I did, he would just get mad and tell me off."

This brief exchange illustrates one of the great human problems. In all kinds of situations people have their feelings hurt by others — they are disappointed, upset, or irritated — but they take great pains to hide their feelings from those who would benefit from knowing how they feel. Probably Mrs. Gray gives off certain signals, intentionally or unintentionally, that let her husband know she is upset. It is quite possible that even though he knows she is upset, he has no idea what he has done to cause it. It is almost impossible for a person to improve unless he knows what he has done wrong.

Why don't people communicate more freely with each other? Why don't children tell their parents about the problems they are having? Why doesn't Mrs. Gray tell her husband what's bothering her?

Perhaps people give off unintentional signals that make someone feel his problems are unimportant and will not be listened to. A child may receive such a message from his parents — or Mrs. Gray, from her husband. But more often the imagined consequences of telling another how we feel are too terrifying, and silence seems to be the safer course.

> Father to daughter: "No, you cannot take the car to pick up Jeannie and go to your class party. You're still too young to drive at night. You can either walk or I'll drive you over. If your teacher can't bring you home, you call and I'll come get you. Also, since it's a school night, be sure to be home by 10:30."
>
> Mary: "Oh, all right, Father." But Mary thinks to herself: "Why is he so unreasonable? Here I am almost seventeen, and I'm the only one of our crowd who can't take the car at night. And it's embarrassing to have to leave the party the earliest of anyone. He treats me like a baby."

The outsider looking at this situation might say that both Mary and her father have some legitimate points in their argument — why don't they talk it over and work out a mutually agreeable solution? Why doesn't Mary tell her father how she feels? Experience may have taught her that her father will not consider her point of view, or that if she speaks up her father will get angry at her for being impertinent. She may be afraid that she'll cry or get too upset, or it could be she has never talked over important things with her father and just doesn't know how. Perhaps she thinks her father will punish her by taking away all her car privileges — or even worse, give her the "cold, silent treatment," accompanied by that hurt, how-could-you-do-this-to-me look.

And the father — why doesn't he talk this over with

his daughter instead of just telling her? Surely he can see (from the silent signals) that she is upset. It could be that he thinks that children should obey parents — not talk back. After all, that's how he was raised by his father. Or perhaps he fears a tearful scene, and he feels that to give the order and retreat behind the newspaper would just be easier and less time-consuming.

Guideposts for Effective Communications

So families often do not talk because of roadblocks in the path of open communications. How can they get rid of these blocks — presuming that they really want to? People and situations are complex and varied, and there are no simple answers, but there are some guideposts from which we might build a strategy to help deal with such situations.

Guidepost 1: Reexamine Your Assumptions

We all assume things about others that may not be true — and we behave as though they were true. How tragic if the assumptions we hold as true are really false! Mrs. Gray assumes that if she tells her husband how she feels, he will "get mad and tell her off." He may have done that once five years ago, and she assumes he is still like that. Mary assumes that if she tries to talk to her father, he will be angry and punish her — but maybe he won't. Wouldn't both Mrs. Gray and Mary do better to assume that the husband or father loves them, wants to have a good relationship, and, if approached in love and kindness, will respond with love and understanding?

Guidepost 2: Take a Risk

In a sense the old adage applies: "Nothing ventured, nothing gained." When we open the communications channels, we sometimes risk the possibility that the other person may become upset or angry and may feel hurt or resentful, but we are also risking the possibility that the

27

situation will improve and the end result will be better. Is the reward worth the risk?

Guidepost 3: Build a Climate of Trust and Understanding

By our actions and expressions we can let others know that we trust and accept them. Parents need to let children know that they will accept their points of view, will listen to their arguments, and will respect their opinions. More than this, the parent needs to say, "I respect you and trust you enough to share my real feelings with you, to confide in you." Sharing begets sharing; openness of communication begets openness from others.

Guidepost 4: Try — And Learn from the Trying

As we take a risk and make a new trial, we may make mistakes. Our communications may be misunderstood, but each trial is a learning experience — we have learned what not to do. Perhaps next time will be better. If others know we are really trying to do better, this may enhance the climate, lessen the risk, and make the next attempt easier and more successful.

Guidepost 5: Keep Talking

The easiest thing to do when our communications are misunderstood or produce the wrong result is to lapse into silence, to avoid the issue, or to pretend it was never said. Usually we have to clear communications channels by adding more communications — in the right kind of climate.

5

MOTIVATE

Why doesn't Mary study more? Will Billy ever get his mind off of model cars and on to math? I guess you could say Ray mowed the lawn — at least he mowed around it. Why can't that boy do a better job?

Questions like these circulate among the sights and sounds in a home and sometimes never find an answer. Parents, unexpectedly thrust into positions as motivators in the family scene, seek answers: How to improve study habits? How to change a given direction? How to *get* somebody going and *keep* him going? How to build motivation into this daydreamer, that procrastinator, and the other slap-dash operator? Not easy questions, and there are no simple answers — but there are some considerations that might be helpful.

Three Motivational Concerns

Parents are concerned with three types of motivation. Examples of each follow:

Direction of Performance

Jeff Jones is a topflight athlete at the age of sixteen. Already he has been a star performer on little league and junior high football, baseball, and basketball teams. He is expected to become a standout in high school. Already he has visions of becoming an All-American.

Ellen Jones, his mother, is worried about Jeff, for she knows that his lack of interest in schoolwork and the resultant low grades may cost him a chance for acceptance at a university. What can she do to encourage Jeff not to neglect his studies?

Ellen Jones faces a problem of *direction change*. How can she help her son shift some of his energies from sports to studies? This is a common motivation concern.

Amount of Performance

It's another failure experience for Tom Johnson, scoutmaster. He has just conducted a board of review for all the scouts in his troop and found that only one out of seventeen boys has earned the merit badges that have been set for them. At this rate none of the boys will reach the Eagle rank, and Tom hopes they all will.

Tom's concern is with *amount* of output. The boys are not doing enough work, and Tom wants to see them increase the number of merit badges they are earning. Leaders in many types of organizations are concerned with motivation for output — wanting to increase the *amount* of performance.

Quality of Performance

Helen Edwards shakes her head sadly as she reads the themes from her English class. She is disappointed in them, for they are generally "rush jobs," trite, filled with errors. She is certain the students are capable of better work than this.

This is a problem of *improved quality*. Helen Edwards's class turns in all the assignments, but the quality of performance is not equal to the potential. Her problem is another common motivational concern — namely, how can one person stimulate others to improve the quality of their performance?

From the point of view of every parent, the above three motivational issues are a rather constant concern. All mothers and fathers are practicing motivators, for all of us deal with the performance of our children and ourselves which needs to be changed in direction, increased, or improved.

Motivation Strategies

How can parents go about motivating their children? How effective are the strategies?

1. Reward-punishment

A common motivation strategy is to offer a reward or threaten a punishment as the basis for performance change. Rewards might include such devices as use of the car, special privileges (staying up late, having a party, going camping), or personal praise. On the other hand, punishment could take the form of loss of privileges, being grounded, a spanking, bad feelings, or loss of favor. Such devices often have mixed results. We find that they work with some people sometimes and not at other times, and sometimes the side effects are disturbing.

Side effects. If the reward or punishment is very important to the person, a reward strategy may be very successful in getting him to change his behavior. One of the side effects can be that he engages in the behavior for the wrong reasons — he studies to get the grade, not to learn the subject; or he works to get the Eagle rank, but not to learn anything about the merit badge subjects.

It may be, when a person's comprehension and experience is limited, that straightforward reward or punishment is understood and facilitates motivation, but later it may lead to resentment, resistance, or performance just good enough to get the reward with no effort to achieve real excellence.

Guilt. A special form of punishment is to engender guilt feelings in a person so he is motivated by trying to reduce the guilt. At times people may need to be reminded of commitments made, promises or pledges which have not been kept. The resultant guilt feeling may

31

indeed cause action, but again for a questionable purpose — to reduce the guilt or to get the guilt-producing person "off my back."

Thus, though reward and punishment may work at times, the problem of the side effects makes it a dubious strategy to employ all the time.

2. *Appeal to the Relationship*

Another motivation device is to use the relationship between people as the basis of change. The classic statement of this kind of appeal is found in the New Testament, where the Master said, "If ye love me, keep my commandments." An increase of commandment keeping would thus be based, not on a fear of reward or punishment, but on identification with the Savior. If we have love for him, we will do what he asks.

Many of us may have been influenced to do something because of a favorite teacher, friend, or parent who asked us to do a certain thing. Because of the feelings in the relationship, we met the request.

Sometimes a person may not truly understand everything about the request but will try to change because of the confidence he has in the other person. This means that the requester must have been trustworthy over a long period of time. It also means that if the relationship changes, the basis of the motivation strategy is lost.

Hidden in the use of the relationship as a motivator may be a threat of some importance. The person may hear that subtle threat, "If you don't do what I ask, I won't like you, and our relationship will be damaged." In such a case the implied punishment of the threat is the great motivator.

3. *Competition*

In our culture a most common motivation strategy is to put people in competition with each other. In one sense this is a variation of the reward method, for it makes people compete for a prize. There is another reward attached, for there is a thrill inherent (for some) in the competition itself and the sense of achievement that comes when one wins. Not all cultures are competitive, however, and some people do not find competition challenging or rewarding.

For competition to be useful, all parties in the competition must be capable of winning some of the time. There are terrible negative effects on a person, or a team, that always loses. When using competition as a motivator, we need always to look at the potential harm done the loser. If the winning becomes more important than the real goal (for example, when boys are more concerned about winning the scout banner than learning about scouting), then competition may be limited in its positive results. Then, too, sometimes people are so threatened by the possibility of losing that they engage in such actions as cheating or lying.

Some systems have been set up in which a person competes against himself and tries to improve on a previous score or record. The effect of such a challenge may level out because a person does not always get better soon enough.

4. Job Enrichment

Another form of motivation is to give people work to do that has within itself the challenge and the reward. It is often remarkable how a rather ordinary man, when he is given a position of responsibility, turns into a magnificent leader. The job itself requires a person to use all his skills; it deals with critical human problems and issues and carries with it a positive motivator of love and respect.

To use this motivator, a parent may have to try to redesign the work or the positions at his disposal. It is not surprising that bright children find no challenge in taking out garbage, making beds, or mowing lawns. It is also interesting how much time and pride they can take in getting the house all ready for a party for their friends. The challenge is to work out enriching activities. Parents living in urban communities have more trouble meeting this challenge than do their country cousins back on the farm, where everyone's work is needed.

One biology teacher began her class each day by sitting and reading. She never gave any assignments or work. For some days the students played and "cut up," but she ignored them. One day a student brought in a bone he had found in a field and asked the teacher what it was. She said, "Let's find out." Together the teacher (and now almost all the students) went through material on fossils and bone structure and discovered what the bone was. Other students began to bring in plants, flowers, and fossils and found the excitement of learning as a process of discovery rather than the drudgery of routine memory work.

5. Commitment

Another motivation strategy is to build into the person his own internal commitment to improve. The motivation comes — not from wanting to obtain a reward (or to avoid a punishment), or to win, or to please someone else — but because the person wants to achieve something he feels is important for him.

True commitment is a difficult condition to achieve and requires great maturity on the part of both the changer and the one who is changing. There are some things that seem to help in this process:

Involvement. People are more committed if they are involved in setting the new goals or making decisions that they will have to implement. Resistance often goes along with the feeling that goals and decisions are being imposed on people when they neither understand them completely nor agree with them.

Understanding. Commitment increases if a person has a real understanding of what he is doing and why he is doing it. It takes more time to communicate real understanding, but the payoff in commitment may be worth the extra time.

Working with. People like to work with others, particularly those in authority, who often want to make assignments and then go off and do their own work. Thus left alone, people seem to lose commitment to the new goal, but if the leader (parent) is there working with them, coaching them, supporting and encouraging and making the new effort meaningful and exciting, then commitment and motivation are increased.

Conclusion

Consider again the problems presented at the beginning of the chapter and ask yourself how Ellen, Tom, and Helen might go about motivating the young people with whom they were dealing. Try to think of specific steps each could begin to take to bring about the desired results.

With a little thought, anyone could apply one or more of the motivational strategies discussed in this chapter in any home situation to begin to change the present motivation — or lack of it — for the better.

6

BE INTER-
DEPENDENT*

"Don't help me, Mother. I want to do it myself," said six-year-old Susie to her mother, who wanted to help her tie her shoes. Almost every child has this early desire to do things on his own, to be competent enough to achieve or accomplish something by himself, not relying on help from anyone else.

"Mother, I can't do it. You've got to help me," called Susie on another occasion, when she was trying to cut out pictures with an awkward instrument called scissors. In this same child is also a need to rely on someone, to depend on another person when she can't manage alone.

Independence versus Dependence

These two crosscurrents seem to be present in all of us — the need to be free, independent, and capable of doing things on our own; and the need to be dependent, to have the right and the luxury of putting ourselves in the hands of others when our own resources are insufficient.

Parents see these apparently conflicting needs in their children, and, depending on their own understanding of themselves and their offspring, they respond in ways that may or may not result in the growth of the child and thus enhance the relationship between the two. It is *from* the parent that the child is trying to break free and demon-

---

*Revised. Reprinted by permission from the *Ensign*, "Interdependence: A family and church goal," February 1971.

strate his own competence, and it is *to* that very parent he goes when he needs support and assistance. Central in the performance of any parent is the manner and method he uses to respond to the needs of his children.

Some parents' style of behavior reinforces and supports the dependency of their children, with the long-range consequence that the child is incapable of functioning adequately on his own. For instance:

> Jane is a college sophomore. She calls home at least three times a week to talk with her parents, to get their advice on her courses, purchases she is going to make, activities she is considering. She feels uneasy and insecure when she has to make a decision before talking with her mother and dad. Her parents are openly pleased with Jane, and they tell their friends with pride that Jane is a real home girl who loves her family — not one of those wild college students. They are glad Jane relies on their judgment and that she so often calls home for advice. They feel needed and important, and their relationship with their daughter is very satisfying to them.

This example points out some of the elements of a strong dependency-development relationship. The persons in the authority positions (in this case the parents) are using the subordinate person (the daughter) to meet many of their own needs. They would probably be indignant and hurt if it were suggested that they are selfish, for being selfish in the sense that they are concerned about themselves at their daughter's expense is not part of their conscious motivation. But in a real sense they are selfish, for they unknowingly have been meeting their own needs without considering the long-range well-being of their daughter.

There are times when dependency is legitimate and useful. Occasions will arise in which a person needs help beyond his own resources. All of us must at times depend on others — doctors, teachers, counselors, repairmen, friends, parents — when conditions face us that are beyond our resources to handle effectively alone. Dependency becomes crippling when a person no longer seeks to develop his own resources or to move to a more collaborative stance with persons in authority, but automatically assumes he cannot do anything without the guidance, support, and influence of others.

All human beings start out in life from a position of almost complete dependency on others. The development of the child away from complete dependency is the responsibility of those adults who occupy positions of authority over him. How to use authority to help that child grow is the major challenge of every parent.

Too often authority persons become concerned with the wrong goals: parents want children who are only well-behaved; teachers want only quiet classrooms or students who will do and say only what the teachers want; administrators want subordinates who will obey without question, who are yes-men. One way to achieve these goals is to create dependency in others. Interestingly enough, many dependency-producing leaders never recognize their part in the problem, for they will often exclaim sadly, "What we need is more people who will take initiative and won't just sit around waiting to be told what to do."

In the other behavioral stream is the desire to be free, to "let me do it by myself." Some have postulated, as did the English philosopher Thomas Hobbes, that the basic nature of man is a condition in which every man is at war with everyone else as each tries to hammer out his own ego-centered world. If everyone actually does only what he wants, without taking others into account, we have anarchy.

As parents see this tendency in their children, they often try to stifle, reduce, or change it. Children don't want to share their toys with others, but parents want them to share. Children don't want to eat certain foods, but mother wants them to clean their plates.

There is a subtle (and sometimes not so subtle) struggle going on between the adults, who want to channel or control, and the youngsters, who want to be independent and free to do as they please. It is this basic struggle that underlies counterdependency. Some people get caught up in a resistance pattern to those in authority and expend much time and energy in finding ways to resist influence over them. They can always find a reason why the desires of the authority person can't or shouldn't be carried out, and they proceed to demonstrate this.

Sometimes this negative response is the result of a wrong approach by the authority, be he parent, teacher, boss, or leader. Perhaps the authority initiates directions to the subordinate in a way that is demeaning and robs him of personal dignity. Often no allowance is made for questions or discussion or dialogue — the parent wants his child to obey "with no back talk." Such an attitude creates in many persons a strong rebellious reaction.

Some parents seem deliberately to create situations where the child questions or resists, so that the parent can "show who is boss" and thus gain a kind of secret delight in dominating another human being.

It should not be assumed, however, that when resistance and reaction occur it is always the fault of the parent. Often the parent may be behaving in a very appropriate manner, but the child has been so conditioned to resent and rebel against authority that, no matter how the parent acts, the child always responds negatively. Sometimes this means that in order to achieve a new and more effective level of interaction, both child and parent need to reexamine their attitudes and behavior and work out a change.

How to Achieve Interdependence

The type of relationship that is both possible and desirable between parent and child is called *interdependence* — the cooperative or collaborative use of each other's resources. Independence is not ideal, for it suggests that the child is freed from those in authority and goes his own way. Independence is not the most effective action in today's world, whether it be in family, school, church, business or government organization, community, nation, or world. Of necessity we are an interdependent people. Unfortunately, most people have not learned to be interdependent with others. From writers and researchers in the field of human behavior we have the following actions that can be taken by one in authority and that will lead toward greater interdependence.

Love and Concern

Every child must know that his parents really care about him, not just that he does what he is told.

Love for the child should be unconditional, although we may not love certain of his actions. Too many parents and other authorities present conditional love as the basis of a relationship: "I will love you only on condition that you do what I want, will be dependent on me, and will meet my needs." Such a basis leads to either dependency or rebellion.

Parents need to talk about their feelings of love and concern with their children. Feelings of the heart need to be shared, no matter how awkward or difficult it may be to do so. And it must be done *now*. Delay only increases the development of the relationship in negative directions.

Trust

Parents need to begin to display greater confidence and trust in their children. They need to trust their children to make correct decisions, and they need to give them that opportunity. The fearful parent is afraid his children will make mistakes or won't do the job just the way he would do it, so he hovers around, watching, checking up, until he makes them feel like the six-year-old fumbling with her shoelaces.

Trust means allowing — allowing children to perform with a sense of confidence that they are supported by their parents. Trust means being consistent and trustworthy so that the child has confidence in the words and actions of the parent.

41

Open Communication

A vital ingredient of interdependence is the open sharing of information. Communication implies that there is a sender and a listener and that there is understanding between the two. In interdependence, both parents and children have a chance to send and to listen. It is not a one-way communication system where the one tells and the other is always supposed to listen. In communication we need to share our thinking and our feelings. On almost every subject or issue people have thoughts, ideas, or opinions as well as feelings. If we want true understanding, we must share both kinds of data.

Many parents share little of their own feelings or ideas with their children. Giving directions, orders, and commands is *not* sharing. Sharing comes first, before the decisions are finally made, and is a process of getting thoughts and feelings out in the open so a good decision can be made.

Before decisions are made, the parent should say, "I want to know what you think and how you feel about the issue at hand. I truly want this information. I will not judge you or punish you for being entirely truthful and candid. If we can both put all our cards on the table, and if we really have concern for each other and trust each other, we can come up with solutions that will be satisfying to all."

Shared Decisions

Interdependence requires that decisions be made in a collaborative way, with all participants understanding each other and coming to a solution they feel good about and are willing to support. Shared decisions are not necessarily fifty-fifty decisions, in the sense that each person will always demand an equal part in everything. Sometimes the father will say, "Son, you have more experience with cars than I do. I trust you to make the decision, and I'll support it." At other times the son will respond similarly to the father. At still other times each

42

will have to listen to the other and work out a solution both can support and implement.

Joint Action

Interdependence means working together. The carrying out of decisions requires that people work together. In too many families, parents tell their children what to do. The parents pressure, control, or punish until the child does what they demand. Too little work is planned and carried out together, with all experiencing the delight of a team effort, the accomplishment of things done collaboratively. Sometimes the work requires effort alone, but it is more satisfying if it can be shared with others.

In our society we see all around us the consequences of young people in rebellion. They are either in revolt against authority or have never learned how to work with authority persons. Training in working together on problem solving and team effort must be taught in the home. This does not mean that parents allow their children license to do whatever they please, nor does it mean that children slavishly carry out the whims of parents; rather, it is a solid condition of mutual effort based on love, concern, and trust.

7

UNDER-STAND FAMILY STYLE

A family, like an individual, develops a personality or a style that characterizes its way of dealing with the issues of family life. In the field of organization research, there is good evidence that under its leaders an organization also develops a certain pattern of functioning that distinguishes it. This pattern often centers around the handling of two major concerns — a concern for work or results and a concern for the people who must do the work or produce the results. The same analysis can be applied to the family. Using the model developed by Blake and Mouton, families could be plotted on the grid on page 47.

The 9-1 Family

The 9-1 family style, particularly as experienced by the children, is one of go-go-go, get the work done: "finish your practicing, school work, housework first, and then we'll see about anything you want to do." It should be emphasized that the completion of work and the accomplishment of goals are important for the growth and satisfaction of family members, but *how* work is done, goals set, priorities established is critical. There is a tendency in the 9-1 family for the parents (sometimes

45

just one) to impose work requirements on family members and constantly push to get things done that others don't understand. Family members may feel that other considerations have not been fairly taken into account, as in the following situation:

> Father: "Children, your mother and I have been talking, and in this time of inflation and shortage we feel that it would be a good thing for the family to grow its own food. We have garden space out in back, and if we all pitch in we can have quite a harvest this fall. What do you think?"
> (Silence)
> Father: "Okay, I think we all agree it would be a good family project. I'll get the seed and rent a roto-tiller to dig up the plot of ground, and we'll get started next Saturday."
> Later the two older boys in the family are talking.
> Tom (age fifteen): "How does Dad come up with all these projects? He says it's a family project, but you know who will get all the blame if it doesn't get done like he wants it. I now have music lessons, schoolwork, scouting merit badges, house and yard work assignments all to get done on Saturday besides this garden. Dad knows I want to play baseball, and the team practices every Saturday. He said he was going to start taking us golfing, but I haven't heard any more about that."
> Bryan (age thirteen): "I hate it when we get into something like this. Dad and Mom will be on us all the time to get that garden weeded or something. All the time they're yelling at us. I'll be glad when I go away to college!"

We find here a family dilemma. A garden is a good project, but the parents (mostly the father) have decided on the project without really talking it over with the children or taking into account other needs the children have. One can predict a continual struggle between parents and children as the father pushes the children to get out and work, and they drag their feet and look for ways to avoid engaging in a project to which they have little commitment. The father may feel he has the well-being of his children in mind, but if they do not experience him as being concerned about them, they are going to behave in various ways that will express their negative feelings: he

46

Blake-Mouton Managerial Grid

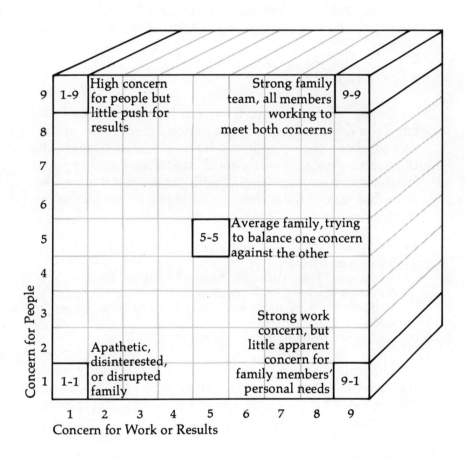

will encounter apathy, resentment, resistance, polite conformity, hostility, and/or rebellion. Again, it is important to remember it is not a "bad" thing for parents to be concerned about work and accomplishment. But if the way they go about it makes their children feel that the *only* thing they are concerned about is external work results, that the children's personal needs and feelings are disregarded, one can predict negative reactions in the family system.

The 1-9 Family

At the other extreme from the highly work-oriented family is the one in which the parents seem to be so concerned about their children's having a good time, liking them, and always "feeling good" that they avoid any confrontation or issue concerned with achievement or results. In such a family the following dialogue would not be uncommon:

> Mother: "Susan, would you come and do the dishes? It's your turn tonight."
> Susan: "I can't tonight, Mom. I promised Sharon I'd come over and we'd study together."
> Mother: "Oh, all right. I guess I can do them for you again."
> Susan: "Thanks, Mom. I'll see you later."

This mother's attitude characterizes the family where the parents are so concerned that their children always "feel good" that they will not deal directly with the necessity for legitimate work. They fear that a confrontation will upset the relationship. The child is clearly in the driver's seat, knows it, and exploits the parental attitude. In the above dialogue the mother probably resents having to do the dishes again and tries to make Susan feel guilty. She probably succeeds but doesn't realize it. At the same time, Susan feels guilty and probably resents her mother for arousing those guilt feelings. The relationship would be healthier if the mother could confront Susan with her resentment of Susan's violation of the agreement to do dishes, and a real resolution could be achieved. It would mean risking the possibility that Susan would be upset for a time. They would have to stand up to each other, and if the mother refused to collapse, Susan would learn to respect her mother's rights and feelings too.

The 1-1 Family

Obviously the most disastrous family is the 1-1 type, where there is little concern exhibited in either direction. It is possible that parents feel concern but for some reason are immobilized and take no action. Sometimes this is a family where people have given up, and each goes his own way, taking care of his own needs. Occasionally in such a family someone — a parent or a child — tries to move toward a new dimension of concern, others become surprised or suspicious, the new behavior is not rewarded, and it is soon abandoned.

Sometimes a family gets into the 1-1 rut because parents want to "run" everything by rules. In such a family parents show no real concern for children or results. The concern is for doing things the "right" way or following traditions or patterns already established that may not now be questioned.

The 5-5 Family

The typical family (if there is such a thing) clusters somewhere around the 5-5 position. There is a conscious effort on the part of parents to take care of both concerns, and there is often a "trade off." This family would push the children on a Saturday to do the housework, mow the lawns, get the work done. Then when the parents feel a little guilty about all the work pressure, they suddenly relent and take the kids out for hamburgers and milkshakes and a drive-in movie.

Families cluster around this position because parents usually ask themselves the wrong question. They think,

"How can *we* get our children to get good things done and yet still take care of their personal needs and concerns?" Always the parents feel it is their responsibility to see that achievement and personal concerns are met. Such situations often develop highly responsible parents but passive, dependent, or even resistant children. Parents expend tremendous energy planning, thinking, worrying about how to get their children to accomplish goals but implicitly assume that it is their problem instead of understanding that the children should be involved in a major part of their own actions. Parents correctly have deep concerns about their children, but their strategies for translating their concerns into action often do not result in the types of responsible behaviors they would like from their children.

J. R. Gibb describes the same problem in school systems when concerned teachers and administrators have often developed inadequate strategies for ensuring the optimum growth of students:

> Somehow, in the process of the development of traditional education, the roles of the student and the teacher have become the reverse of what they should be in participative education. The student should be the primary participant. In traditional education the teachers do what the students should do and the students act as disinterested observers of the process. The college frequently becomes an institution where the students pay tuition to subsidize the teachers, who do the learning. This topsy-turvy condition is well evidenced by a kind of job analysis of the teacher activities. The teacher robs the student of each of these vital experiences: he sets the goals for the students, formulates the questions and problems, evaluates progress, organizes the experience of the student, "integrates" the curriculum, plans the course and the lectures, thinks about the course problems outside of class hours, and does most of the talking. In short, the teachers are the students, the learners, the *participants* in the educative process. It is common-place to hear teachers say: "I never learned so much as in my first year of teaching." It is questionable how long our society can support institutions where "students" sit and watch teachers learn (1951:65).

The 9-9 Family

The ideal family in this model is the 9-9 type, in which both work and human concerns thrive. Probably few families achieve such a condition all the time, but it represents a goal towards which any family may strive.

Strategies for Showing Concern

What makes a 9-9 family different from the 5-5 if the 5-5 parents already have full concern? The strategy for implementing the concern is the major factor. Parents in the 9-9 family ask themselves, "What are the conditions we need to create in the family so that *all of us* will not only feel responsible for the family but will take appropriate action?" The 9-9 family is revealed in a feeling among all family members that they are part of a *team*, and each feels responsible to see that the team succeeds. In an effective team there are not five captains or eleven quarterbacks or three head coaches. Each understands and respects the position, authority, and responsibilities of the others, but every person feels that he must do his part or the effort will not be successful. Everyone on the team is concerned about the work and about helping each other. Thus in a 9-9 family, all family members feel a sense of responsibility for the well-being of all the others, and they work together to see that each achieves.

Here is an example of a 9-9 family in action:

It's a Monday evening, and the family are all seated about the dining-room table in a family council. Dad has the floor and is talking about finances: "You are all aware that inflation is skyrocketing, and my salary isn't matching it. My take home pay is $985.73 per month (I don't think I need to remind you that our discussion of personal family matters is confidential), and we are just about breaking even. This fall members of our family start in college. Stan is the first to go, and he has saved nearly a thousand dollars, but the total expense will be close to three thousand dollars for the year. He will try to get a part-time job, but they're scarce. This means that we will have to help Stan

51

with between $100 and $150 per month. I can't do that unless we all help. How can we cut down expenses or get more income to help Stan go to college?"

There was a short pause. Sherry, the sixteen-year-old oldest girl said, "It would help if I started sewing more of my own clothes." Others began to make suggestions: "I'll get a job after school." "Turn off the lights and save electricity." "Let's plant a garden."

Team-building Actions

This father has the fundamental idea about the family as a team, and he engages in appropriate actions.

1. *Data sharing.* He levels with the family, letting them know exactly what the situation is, what his salary is, and what is needed. A real team needs to have clear, accurate information to make good decisions.

2. *Free, informed choices and decisions.* Based on information, the family members need to make their own decisions as to what they are willing to do. Commitment is in part a function of one's involvement and participation in making a decision that will affect his own life.

3. *Commitment to follow through and implement decisions.* A real team will make sure that it carries out its decisions. There will be deadlines set, schedules outlined, assignments made, and times for reporting progress set up. The ineffective team gets bogged down in implementing, and the lack of follow-through sees many a good idea lost.

4. *Basic concern.* Underlying the whole effort is the feeling that each member is truly concerned about the other members. Each wants the others to grow, to achieve, and each is willing to extend effort to translate his concern into concrete action.

Not all families are going to achieve a 9-9 style the same way, and 9-9 families may look quite different from the outside.

Mixed Parental Styles

The personal styles of a father and a mother may be quite different, yet the combination could be highly complementary. It often occurs that one parent — the mother — is 9-1 oriented; that is, she has strong feelings about goal accomplishment and is highly task-centered. She tends to be the prime mover in the family towards achievement and excellence in performance. The father could be 1-9 in his style, concerned with building and maintaining relationships, tending feelings, and providing emotional support. This mixture could be a complementary blend or a witch's brew. If the mother resents the father's relationship-building activities or if the father fails to support his wife's efforts towards achievement, there will be struggle and conflict — either open or under cover — and all will suffer. But if the father can lend support to accomplishment, be a silent signal of strength to work well done, the mother will be helped to achieve good things. She must also be a partner in appreciating the father's contribution in keeping the relationships mended and in tune.

Families can change. Parents of many different mixes of personal styles can say, "We don't like the way we are. Let's do something better." The important factor is mutual desire to change, setting new goals, and beginning to engage in different activities.

Back-up Styles

In their original discussion of their model, Blake and Mouton describe people who have a preferred style, but who, if that doesn't work directly, revert to a more primitive back-up style. A family might want to be 9-9; that is, they try to work together as a team, to plan together and work together. However, if some family member(s) does not respond as expected, parents can revert to a 9-1 back-up style. Direct threat or coercion now comes into play as the demand for accomplishment takes precedence.

Or it is possible that a 1-9 back-up style moves forward, and the task is forgotten or at least dropped, in the interest of keeping the child content in the family system. Parents may also have a 1-1 back up style; that is, when things do not go as expected or planned, they retreat into inactivity and sit helplessly doing nothing.

Time for a Change?

Whatever your family style, it could be discussed and the grid studied together in a family meeting. Such a discussion would result in a clearer understanding of where you are now as a family and where you'd like to be. Perhaps specific suggestions could be made, considered, and put into action about how to get there.

8

DEAL
WITH FEELINGS

Good-bye at the Airport

It's the week after Christmas, and the airport is jammed with people returning home after vacations with their families. Two groups of people — apparently two families — are clustered together engaging in that last bit of talk that precedes good-bye. Children of similar ages talk rapidly together. Then comes the final announcement for boarding the aircraft. The two mothers — apparently sisters — kiss each other as the men clasp hands warmly. Then the two boys, about ten years old, say good-bye and burst into tears. They throw their arms around each other and cling together, sobbing all the while. Tears flow, not only from the family, but from many an observer touched by the open show of affection and love by two little boys for each other.

In some way the parents of these boys have helped them understand that the expression of honest emotion, even in public, is something not to be ashamed of or avoided.

Someone has said that the two great capabilities that distinguish man from the lower animals are his thinking and feeling within a broader range. Yet many people run into difficulty as they try to manage these two great abilities. Some subordinate one to the other; others deny the feeling component except in rare bursts of emotionalism. Many hide and emerge timidly in the emotional range, feeling fearful and anxious lest they reveal the powerful forces pent up behind some inner dike. There are some who give themselves over to emotionalism and live hedonistic lives, subordinating thinking to the demands of their feelings.

How can family members help each other learn to live healthily and productively with human feelings and to achieve a balance between reason and emotion?

Denying Feelings

Recent evidence indicates that among American businessmen there has been a strong emphasis on organizing one's life along rational lines accompanied with a denial of the importance of dealing with the feeling component of human behavior. A study by Argyris showed a unanimous preference on the part of administrators for trying to deal with problems on a rational basis only and for avoiding, at almost all cost, the handling of feelings and emotions. Something in the training of these executives led them to a conviction that trying to deal with feelings is disturbing and consequently unwise. They therefore denied feeling data as unrealistic or assumed that they were not competent to deal with feelings. Such an attitude on the part of a father would undoubtedly be communicated to his children, and one might expect that it would tend to block off any expression of the emotional component in the family.

All family members — parents and children — will inevitably experience nearly the whole range of human emotion — love, anger, frustration, anxiety, fear, hate, jealousy, irritation, tenderness, and all the rest. How in the family setting can one provide the experience and training for learning to cope with these feelings productively? Inability to do so could lead to the development of personalities with a range of unbalanced behavioral characteristics. One such characteristic would be to deny

all feelings; another, to suffer from psychosomatic ill-
nesses caused by suppressed emotions. One person might
be a stern represser of feelings; someone else might furi-
ously unleash his emotions in almost uncontrolled reactions. Families are well advised to develop a theory and
a method for coping with the boundless emotions that
will occur.

Accepting Feelings

Haim Ginott, the popular writer on parent-child relations, emphasized strongly in his writings the importance
of adult acceptance of the reality of the feelings of children. This does not mean one likes or approves the feelings — or particularly the behavior stemming from an
emotional condition — but one accepts the fact that feelings do exist. A first principle in coping with feelings is to
admit them, accept them as real, and then develop ways of
handling them.

If a child is told, "You shouldn't feel like that," or "I
can't believe you really feel that way," or "Quit feeling
like that. Act like a man," he is not receiving any help in
learning to cope with his feelings of anger. Such responses often result in children's hiding their real feelings
from their parents, feeling guilty when they have such
emotions, and worrying about the terrible things that
might occur if such feelings were ever admitted or expressed. Children can also use their feelings as a control
measure — the way to get parents concerned or upset.
They may learn that the way to get their parents' un-
divided attention is to become emotional and threaten
some kind of upheaval. One insightful writer counsels as
follows:

> School thy feelings, oh my brother,
> Train thy warm, impulsive soul;
> Do not its emotion smother,
> But let wisdom's voice control.
> [Charles W. Penrose, "Feelings"]

Here is suggested an important interplay between emotion and thinking. One does not deny or "smother" the feeling part of one's life, but the rational portion of oneself is allowed to intervene and mediate the feelings.

Feelings of anger, resentment, or hate are the violent emotional responses so frightening to people that they often hide, repress, or deny them. Perhaps there is the unconscious terror that if such feelings are not immediately squelched, they might be acted out with disastrous consequences.

Expressing Emotional Reactions

Alternatives to both suppression and full enactment are suggested in the following real-life story:

> Allan was furious. He had paid eighteen dollars of his own money to buy a new knit sportshirt, and after he had worn it only once, here it was crumpled on the floor with a spot on the front. He was positive that his younger brother, James, had worn it without his permission. To add insult to injury, he had now not only soiled it but had failed to hang it up.
>
> With blood in his eye, Allan went searching for his victim like an angel of doom. When he found James watching TV, he jumped on him with a shriek and began to pound the now screaming younger boy. Mother was soon at the scene and with some difficulty separated her sons. Allan was almost sobbing with anger, and James was on the verge of tears from fear and need for defense and revenge.
>
> "What in the world brought this on?" asked mother.
>
> "I hate James," Allan said through clenched teeth. "I feel like killing him."
>
> "Wanting to kill is a pretty strong feeling, Allan. Why do you feel like that?"
>
> The story came flowing from the older boy in the river of his anger. After listening to all of it, mother said, "James, can you understand how Allan feels and why he would feel that way?"
>
> Immediately James rose to his own defense. "That's no reason for him to come down and start hitting me," he said. "Besides, he said I could wear his shirt sometimes."
>
> Mother replied, "James, you'll get your chance to ex-

plain your side, but right now I want to see if you can understand how Allan feels. He thinks that you unfairly wore his shirt without asking, soiled it, and left it lying on the floor. He was very proud of that shirt since he bought it with his own money, and now he feels extremely angry and upset about it. Can you understand how he feels?"

"Yeah, I guess so," muttered James.

Mother continued, "Allan, we both can understand how you feel, but when you jump on James and start hitting him, I can tell he begins to feel both frightened and angry in return and wants to fight back. Is that really what you want?"

This mother is performing a useful function as a third party, helping the boys deal with their feelings. She has not condemned Allan for feeling angry, but she does want him to examine his behavior, the expression of his feelings, to see if that expression is the most appropriate outlet for his emotional state. She wants to help her son see that there are alternative ways to express his feelings.

Perhaps he can learn to express his feelings of irritation and upset directly to his brother without either hitting him or suppressing and harboring ill feelings that could be fed by any further provocation. It may also be possible for Allan to learn not to react immediately to a situation. As he learns to combine thought and feeling, he may learn to hold his emotional outbursts in abeyance until he gathers all the information he needs. Had he done so in this instance, he might have learned that his brother honestly thought he had permission to wear the shirt, that he knew it was spotted, and that he planned to get it cleaned and was therefore not concerned that the shirt was crumpled on the floor. One does not always need to react emotionally immediately. Thinking can be a mediating influence without robbing one of the richness of the world of feelings.

Stormy, negative, or destructive feelings may need to be cushioned or mediated by the thinking process. It is not necessary, useful, or desirable to act out every emotional state. To do so would result in emotional anarchy. People can learn to wrestle with their own feelings and to decide, on the basis of a priority system of values, not to respond violently to the immediate emotion. One can share his feelings — that is, talk about them, describe them to others, without acting them out. You may feel like hitting or cursing someone toward whom you have negative feelings, but if you tell that person how you feel, the need for actually hitting or cursing is diminished.

Whether a person acts out his feeling state would depend on the degree to which the acting out would allow him to be consistent with his most important values. If a father held to the value of loving his wife and children and wanting to see their lives enriched and filled with growth opportunities, it would be a denial of those values if he abused or ridiculed them in a devastating way — even though he was momentarily angry with them.

Showing Feelings of Love

It is not only the strong negative or destructive feelings that concern people, but also the warm, positive love feelings. Some people learn to hide all negative emotions or keep them bottled up inside, and others learn to smother their feelings of love and affection. There is the old story of the Scotsman who at the funeral of his wife choked, "She was a wonderful woman, and I came close to telling her that once or twice."

Tevye in *Fiddler on the Roof* asks his wife, "Do you love me?" After some reflection, she admits she does, and he remarks, "After twenty-five years, it's nice to know."

For some it is extremely difficult to express love and affection openly. Families may unconsciously develop a tradition either for warm sharing or for restricted reaction. For the latter, it would be an embarrassing violation of family custom for a son to hug his father or kiss his sister, even though he might want to. It is not necessary for all families to be openly demonstrative, but families should examine carefully whether they are too restrictive. People can become more open in their expressions of love — to the delight of others. It is not too much of a risk to begin to respond to our love feelings more spontaneously and to share them with those we truly cherish.

9

DON'T DECIDE TO FAIL*

The Trip to Abilene: A Modern Parable

A young man and his bride are visiting her parents in the town of Coleman, Texas. Coleman is in the middle of the plains, where the wind blows, and it gets hot. It is the middle of summer, and there is not much to do in Coleman, a town of about five thousand. So the young man, his wife, and his parents-in-law are sitting around on a Sunday afternoon, drinking lemonade and playing dominoes. From all appearances, the family is having a good time, when suddenly and surprisingly the father-in-law says, "Why don't we all get dressed and drive to Abilene, and have dinner in the cafeteria?"

The young man thinks to himself, "Good night, there is nothing I would like to do less than to drive to Abilene." Abilene is fifty-three miles from Coleman, over a winding road. He knows that the car does not have air conditioning, and in order to keep the wind from blowing the dust all all over them, they will have to drive with the windows up. He also knows that the only cafeteria open in Abilene on a Sunday afternoon is the Good Luck Cafeteria, where the food leaves much to be desired. But he thinks, "If my father-in-law wants to go to Abilene, I guess it's all right." So he says, "That sounds fine to me. I mean if Beth (his wife) wants to go."

---

*With Jerry B. Harvey.

And she says, "Well, yes, if everyone wants to go to Abilene, that's fine; if Mother really wants to go."

Mother replies, "Oh yes, if you all want to go, well, that's where I want to go."

They all put on their Sunday clothes, climb into the old Buick, and take the long, hot, dusty trip to Abilene. When they arrive there, sure enough, the only place open is the Good Luck Cafeteria. They have a greasy meal, crowd back into the car, and drive the miserable fifty-three miles home. Finally, worn out, hot, dusty, irritable, they stagger back into the house and have another glass of lemonade.

The father-in-law sighs, "Boy, am I glad that's over. If there's anything I didn't want to do, it was to go to Abilene. I sure wouldn't have gone if you three hadn't pressured me into it!"

His son-in-law retorts, "What do you mean, you didn't want to go to Abilene? And what do you mean, we pressured you into it? I only went because the rest of you wanted to go. I didn't pressure anybody."

Beth speaks up, "What do you mean? I didn't want to go to Abilene. The only reason I went was because you, Mama, and Daddy wanted to go."

Mother chimes in, "I didn't want to go to Abilene. That was the last place in the world I wanted to go. I only went because Father and the two of you wanted to go."

Father expands on his previous statement, "As I said before, I didn't want to go to Abilene. I just suggested going because I was afraid everybody was really bored sitting around playing dominoes, and I thought you might prefer to do something else. I was just sort of making conversation, hoping you'd suggest something better, but I really didn't expect you to take me up on my idea."

The Abilene Paradox

The above story represents an interesting paradox: four reasonably intelligent people all combining to do something that none of them wanted to do in the first place. In fact, as a paradox within a paradox, you might say that their inability to cope with agreement (that is, the hidden agreement that they didn't want to go to Abilene) was the basic cause of their dilemma.

That is the parable. Like any parable, it suggests many interpretations and many lessons to be learned. You

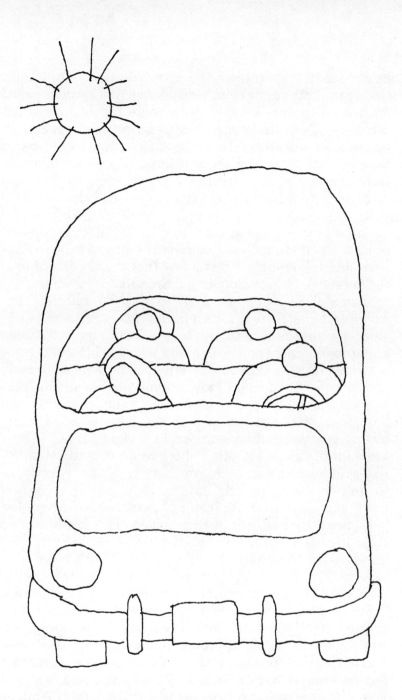

They all put on their Sunday clothes, climb into the old
Buick, and take the long, hot, dusty trip to Abilene.

might see in it a problem in communication. You might find fear. You might even see some mental conflict based on love. Perhaps you will draw some conclusions about integrity. Of central concern is an action in which each of us, individually and collectively, may engage from time to time — that is, taking an unwanted trip to Abilene. In fact, one of the primary functions of effective management of families, churches, businesses, and governments is to keep people from taking a dusty trip to Abilene and eating a greasy meal at the Good Luck Cafeteria. Stated differently, there are many different kinds of trips to Abilene, and following are just a few that may be possible at the personal, interpersonal, and organizational levels.

Some occur as people make critical life choices. For example, a marriage can turn into a trip to Abilene. Consider a young man and a young woman who have been going together for some time and who are planning to be married. If you were to interview each of them separately and privately and ask, "How do you feel about this person you have selected?" the answer might be something like this: "Honestly, now that you have asked, I really feel deep down that he (she) isn't the right person. There are a lot of things we don't share or do or understand or like about each other." Unfortunately, like many couples, to bolster a sagging relationship they may have moved more and more into the realm of personal intimacy. Expectations are built up in themselves, their families, and their friends, until it becomes difficult — at least in their minds — to terminate the relationship. Both have been talking about getting married although neither really wants to or feels it is the right thing to do. The girl thinks, "He is expecting to go through with this." The boy says to himself, "I am sure she is planning the wedding." If you ask them, "What are you going to do about this situation?" they will probably say, "We are going to announce our wedding date next week." This would be a case of a young couple in danger of taking a tragic trip to Abilene by doing something that neither wants to do and by engaging in an activity and making a crucial decision that neither feels is appropriate. One might say they are making a decision to fail.

Another kind of trip to Abilene might involve the choosing of an occupation or a life-style. For example, someone might ask a recent college graduate, "What do you want to do, now that you have your degree?" and he, searching deep within himself, might reply, "You know, what I'd really like to do is to go buy a farm, raise some cattle, teach high school, and work in the Boy Scouts."

"What are you going to do?"

"Well, next week I am going to Los Angeles to accept a job in the aerospace industry."

If he carries through with such a decision, he would for all intents and purposes consign himself to an endless series of meals at the Good Luck Cafeteria.

Not all students make such a poor choice. Recently, for instance, a student who had received a master of business administration degree wrote a letter to his professor. He described finishing his degree and added, "I was at this time contemplating traveling to any number of metropolitan areas to find work since my search at school left me jobless. Instead I took a construction job in Grand Teton National Park with hopes in mind of being able to latch onto something in that area. At the summer's end I received an offer and took a job in park management, still in Grand Teton. I have had a chance to think throughout the quiet winter evenings, and I realize that I am much happier than I would have been surrounded by the noise and bustle of city life. I have also come to realize that I just was not cut out for the keen competitive life of high finance and am thoroughly enjoying the more leisurely approach to life that is offered in the National Park Service. Being located in an area that is only five miles to work and less than fifty yards into the woods makes up for whatever else might be lacking in the way of culture and erstwhile eases of life that are found in the big city." Here is at least one young man who avoided a dusty trip to Abilene. Everyone need not live on the farm or in the woods to avoid taking the trip. There are some who, if they were to search the deeper recesses of their own thoughts and their own aspirations, would say, "I really want to be a writer, or I have the capability of being a topflight scientist. I really should get a Ph.D." But their trip to Abilene would be taking the nearest, most available job at the best salary, which would put them where they don't want to be, joining that fellow in the aerospace industry for a greasy meal at the Good Luck Cafeteria.

Some who are married find a trip to Abilene in their own relationship. Too often is this true with couples who have begun to move in directions that neither desires. If you were to talk to each of them privately, the interview would go something like this:

With the young wife, "How do you feel about your relationship?"

"I'm not too satisfied or happy."

"What's the matter?"

"We don't really do a lot of things together. We seem to be drifting away from our basic values. We tend to bicker and quarrel and fight with each other more than we should."

"You're not satisfied with that?"

"No, I don't like it at all."

Likewise, if you talk with the young husband, he would say much the same thing: "I don't like it. I'm not satisfied with what we are doing. I don't really like the direction we are going. It isn't what I want."

"What are you going to do about it?"

"Well, we'll probably sit in the front room and quarrel and fight, and go to bed and sulk." They are indeed taking a trip to Abilene when Salt Lake City or San Bernardino is where they would rather be.

A striking piece of research in the field of social psychology was done by a professor at Yale, Stanley Milgram, who presents what can be a dangerous kind of trip to Abilene for anyone. He decided to investigate the possibility that people may give up their responsibility for decision to others in positions of authority. To test his basic hypothesis, he invited college students into a laboratory. When they arrived, they would see a man seated in what appeared to be an electric chair with electrodes attached to his body. What the students didn't know was that the chair was a fake; no electricity actually came in.

The experimenter would announce, "We want to see how much electric shock this person can take. Would you sit down at the control board and manipulate that central knob which will shock the person with increasing amounts of electricity." The student would sit down, and the experimenter would say, "Turn the switch." The student would turn the switch. A light would go on in front of the person in the electric chair, and he would begin to scream and writhe in pretended pain. The student could see and hear him. He would look up, and the experimenter would say, "That's all right, he can take more. Give him some more." The student would turn the knob more, and the person in the chair would yell and scream harder and louder. Again the student would look up, and the experimenter would say, "That's all right; he can take more; give it to him." A large percentage of students would continue to turn the knob more and more and more, even though they could see and hear the apparent evidence of their own action.

When the experiment was over the interviewers asked, "Why did you do it? Didn't you see the person was in pain?"

"Yes, I saw it," was the common answer.

"Why did you continue?"

The reply was simple: "It wasn't my experiment; after all it was the psychologist who was in charge. I figured he knew what he was doing, so I just followed what he said." Anytime any person ignores his own conscience, violates his own values, and begins to engage in behavior that he personally feels is not right or conscionable or appropriate, he is in danger of taking a terrible trip to Abilene.

Since we find people taking trips to Abilene at the family and the individual level, we are compelled to ask,

69

Why? What is it that causes people to marry people they don't love, take jobs they don't like, and support actions of which they disapprove? Stated differently, why do they make decisions to fail? Underlying all such decisions is fear mingled with fantasy — the fear of what might happen if one speaks up and voices the truth as he sees it. What will people say if we break our engagement? What will my wife say if I admit that I haven't been planning our family life the way I think she wants it? What will people around me say if I don't go ahead and take the job in Chicago? What will happen to me if I stand up and admit that the last decision we made was bad and ineffective? What will happen to me if I go against prevailing political opinion? Fear colored by the fantasy of what might happen if we don't keep our mouths closed can put us in danger of climbing into a car and taking a long, dusty, pointless trip to Abilene when we might prefer to be in New Orleans.

Avoiding Trips to Abilene

Since a major characteristic of a decision to fail is an unawareness of the real feelings of others, it is important that someone take enough risk to voice his concerns and put them out in the open in front of others.

Regardless of whether the person is in a business organization, a family, or a church, he must accept the consequences of his risk. Others hearing his declaration of what he honestly feels may be encouraged to overcome their fears and fantasies. As a result of the new, honest information, they all may find they are on a road none wants to travel. Thus would arise the opportunity to change their course in a direction they really want to go. It is also possible the person raising the issue for open consideration may find there is real disagreement with his concern, and in that case he may set his fears at rest. There is also the possibility that the others are so afraid to reverse their previous decisions that they will react negatively to the person who has raised their secret fears to the

70

level of discussion and examination. He may be penalized in some way, or even rejected; but at the same time he will be forced to move in directions that express his honest commitments.

The parent, family member, or friend who discovers the dynamics of hidden agreement inherent in the Abilene paradox will serve others best by bringing all parties together and identifying for everyone the major agreements he has heard. He may even tell the Abilene parable and ask those present if the data he has gathered represent such a possibility for them. Having brought the basic agreements to the surface, he tries to help everyone involved to reduce the anxiety, stemming from phantom fear and fantasies, which blocks problem solving and to come to grips with making the decisions and taking the actions that such honest agreement requires. In summary, by focusing on hidden agreements, it may be possible to help others reach conclusions which succeed rather than decisions which fail.

10
TRUST

A mother was talking with a high school principal: "I just can't seem to do anything with Tom anymore, Mr. Bickmore. We used to talk together a lot, but now he has become defiant and rebellious. We seem to be fighting all the time. I know that since he has been in high school he has been more tense and nervous than before. He hides things from me, won't tell me where he's going or what he's doing. I'm afraid that he might get into some kind of trouble, and I know he's not doing well in school. What can I do?"

The principal thought for a few moments before he replied, "Well, Mrs. Scott, Tom may have some problems that he doesn't feel free to talk about with you. If you could build more of a feeling of trust with him, perhaps he would begin talking with you again. My advice is to work on improving the feelings of confidence and trust between the two of you."

The principal was probably right. Something was wrong in Tom's family, and the advice to "work on" the relationship was good. The major question, however, remained unanswered: How do you go about building a trust relationship with another person?

One of the most common clichés used in talking about the basis for working effectively with other people is that you must first "build a good relationship," "develop rapport," "establish a good climate," or "gain their confidence." Too often the discussion stops at this point as though the subject were covered when the principle is stated. Each person is left to his own devices as to what should be done in establishing a critical base for the whole subsequent relationship.

The Basis for Trust

When someone says, "I trust you," what does he usually mean?

Honesty

A critical dimension is honesty. To trust is to have confidence that another person's word is an accurate representation of what he will do. It is hard to trust a person who says one thing and does another. Underlying all trust relationships is the willingness to put something of oneself into another's care. No one wants to impart his secrets or confidences to a person who will not keep them. Who would knowingly invest his time, energy, and resources in the making of a decision with someone who would not follow through on the agreement made? Honesty or integrity is basic to a relationship of trust, a sense that one can count on another person to do what he says he will do.

Members of families are often not aware of the things they do that destroy trust. It doesn't take many incidents like these to erode away what is thought to be a firm foundation of trust:

> "Dad, will you come and play ball with me?"
> "Sure, son, just as soon as I finish what I'm doing."
> One hour later: "Dad, aren't you going to come and play ball like you said?"
> "I'm sorry, son, but I got busy doing something else; we'll play ball another time."
>
> Dad: "Ann, I hear that you've got a new boyfriend — only he doesn't know about it yet. I think I'll call him up

74

and tell him to watch out for you."

Ann (to her mother): "Mother, how could you tell Dad when you said you wouldn't say anything to anybody?"

Mother: "Oh, it doesn't matter if your Dad knows. After all, he's only kidding about calling him up."

Often a harried parent, pressured by his child, will make a promise he has no intention of keeping, in order to get some "peace and quiet."

Sally: "Mother, today's the day of that big sale on girls' pants that you said we could go to."

Mother: "Don't bother me, Sally. I'm making these cookies for Mrs. Johnson, and then I have to go to a meeting."

Sally: "But, Mother, you promised — "

Mother: "That's enough, Sally. I just can't make it today."

Of course, sometimes there will be unexpected interruptions to the best-laid plans, and a child needs to learn to adjust his demands. When the pattern, however, is one of broken promises, the base of trust is chipped away.

Some parents suppose that, when the child does not mention the matter again, he has forgotten it, and so the strategy worked. Each parent would do well to operate from another assumption: A child remembers more than I think, and any violation of my word eats at the foundation of my trust relationship with him.

Caring

Fundamental to a trust relationship is the feeling one person has that another person "cares" for him. Caring is equated with concern for or interest in someone else. It is not the same as liking or affection. It is possible to have feelings of affection for a person you don't basically trust, and as a result you hold back some things about yourself from that person.

The feeling of being cared for is a very subtle quality, as illustrated in the following story:

Two high school couples are going on a double date to a school dance. After the dance, they go to a local cafe for something to eat. Eating and talking, they forget about the time. About 1:30 Joan's mother suddenly appears at their booth. She is in her nightgown with a coat thrown over her shoulders. Looking directly at her daughter, she says, "I told you that if you were not home by 1:00, I was coming after you. Come with me, young lady." And with that she marches Joan out of the cafe and home.

The next day Joan and Cindy meet and talk. Joan is terribly mortified about her mother's actions, but Cindy's reaction is interesting. She says, "I wish my mother cared enough about me to come and get me. She doesn't care what I do or when I come home."

On the face of it neither of the two mothers was building a real trust relationship. Joan felt that her mother did not trust her, and this lack of feeling trusted might erode their relationship even though her mother seemed to care about her. On the other hand, Cindy's mother may have been trying to display trust in her daughter by not questioning her actions, but Cindy interpreted her behavior as a lack of caring.

There is a fine interplay between these two qualities — caring and placing trust in others. People need to be shown that someone is concerned about the consequences of their actions and is willing to invest something of himself in terms of time, intimacy, and personal warmth to show that concern. A common phrase used to indicate a lack of concern for another person is "I couldn't care less." If one member of a family feels that others in the family are not concerned enough about him to invest any of their own personal resources in his behalf, it would be predicted that trust will be low. The investment of personal resources means giving up something of real value on behalf of the other person. Many parents with money give money to their children but reserve their more precious resources, such as time, warmth, and intimacy, expecting nevertheless to have a close, trusting relationship with their children. Parents should assume that children are able to distinguish between the giving of something of personal worth and the giving of something that does not represent a real investment of self.

Learning to Trust Others

Mutual Confidence

If trust is to be built between people, then a mutuality of confidence must be exchanged. It is virtually impossible to build a trust relationship if one party in the relationship says in effect, "I want you to trust me and to have a trust relationship, but I don't really trust you to keep your word, to show judgment, or to be responsible. I am trustworthy, but you are not."

Often this is what parents communicate to children when they "check up" on them. Consider the following:

> Mother: "Susan, I want you in by 1:00 a.m. after your date tonight. Is that agreed?"
> Susan: "All right, Mother, I'll be in then."
> Mother: "Just to make sure that you're in, I'm going to set my alarm for 1:00. If you're in by then, just snap the alarm off; but if you're not in, then I am going to get up and we'll just have to see what happens."

This mother is saying in effect, "Daughter, you say you will be on time, but I don't really trust you to be honest or responsible; so I am going to check up to make sure." This mother might say that the only reason she would set the alarm is that she is concerned, and checking up is just showing concern. Here again is that sensitive balance between showing concern and showing confidence or trusting another person. In some families there seems to be an assumption that a person is untrustworthy until he proves he can be trusted. A trust relationship would probably develop more easily from the opposite premise: that a person is considered trustworthy until proven otherwise. At least the latter view is consistent with our notions of guilt and innocence.

Suppose in the above situation that the daughter and her date had flat tire or were detained for some other

77

legitimate reason. The setting of the alarm clock will not change that, but it might alert the mother to mobilize some help — and this is usually given as the reason for a check-up system. Actually the method means the mother must allow the daughter to cope with any unexpected situation in her own way since the mother is out of the picture until the alarm goes off.

Or suppose the daughter *is* untrustworthy. Evidence from research points out that a check-up system is no real deterrent to untrustworthy people. In fact, they almost invariably try to "beat" the system. An untrustworthy daughter could come in, snap off the alarm, and then sneak back out. The mother would then have to think up another way to check up on her daughter which the daughter would probably try to beat. Thus there would be a constant strategy-counterstrategy game going on between mother and daughter — the exact opposite of a trust relationship.

It is often extremely difficult for parents to trust a child to make wise decisions when they are fairly sure the decision the child makes will be different from their own under the same circumstances. Does trusting another person, particularly a child, mean that he is allowed to do whatever he wants to do? Trusting at that point is entwined closely with freedom. How much freedom and autonomy can we entrust to a child? Parents are constantly fearful that their children will make mistakes that will have long-range, painful consequences; and as a result they are afraid to allow them too much freedom. But maturity and judgment come as a child learns to make decisions and to profit from his own experiences. It is not good child training for a parent to make all the choices, eliminating the child's right to experiment and learn. He needs to learn to use freedom wisely and to become trustworthy so that when he becomes an adult he is able to make choices and decisions on his own.

It is possible for a parent to have the type of relationship with a child where there is a real confidence between them, a sense of trust and concern, a mutuality of sharing, an openness of communication. Then the child seeks the opinions and experiences of the parents, and almost anything can be discussed openly and freely. Out of that free exchange, the child makes his own decisions with a degree of confidence, knowing that he has gathered adequate data and that his decisions will be respected by his parents.

Openness

An important part of building trust is developing a system of openness in communication. It is difficult for anyone to trust someone else who will not tell him everything important to know about situations of mutual concern. Openness has at least two dimensions: *sharing* — letting others know our personal thoughts, ideas, opinions, feelings, experiences, and reactions; and *leveling* — being honest and candid in letting others know how we feel about them and their behavior.

Some families have very little sharing; that is, they do not share their daily experiences, troubles, concerns, or joys with each other. Parents often want their children to share with them but do very little sharing in return. A common dinner-table conversation goes something like this:

> Dad: "Well, Bob, how was school today?"
> Bob: "OK, I guess."
> Dad: "Tell me what happened today. Anything interesting?"
> Bob: "Nah, just the same old stuff."
> Dad to Mother: "It's like pumping water out of a dry well trying to get any information out of that boy."

What the father should realize is that he has probably shared very little of his day with anyone. In fact, much the same conversation probably took place between Mother and Dad when he came home, and she wanted to find out how his day went.

Just as caring begets caring, and trusting elicits trusting, so does sharing bring forth more sharing. If one family member can begin to share more of himself with others, it will open the way for the others to share. Each will then begin to feel that other family members trust him enough to share things of real concern and importance with him. Almost every child can recall times when he has come upon his parents in a discussion that is abruptly halted as soon as he comes into the room. He can probably remember, too, his curiosity and the temptation to eavesdrop to find out what he wasn't supposed to hear. Perhaps there are some sensitive matters that might not be appropriate for children at some ages, but if a child senses that his parents are constantly filtering or screening out the conversation, feelings that the parents do not trust him begin to develop. He learns to be careful of what he says in return, and a low sharing relationship begins to develop.

Leveling is a specific form of sharing — namely, letting another person know how we feel about his behavior.

A wife says to her husband, who has just come home from work, has completely ignored her, and is sitting in the front room reading the paper, "John, when you come home and don't even come in to tell me hello, it makes me feel very angry and resentful toward you. I feel like punishing you in some way." She is letting her husband know *what he has done* by describing his behavior and *how it makes her feel* by describing her inner state of feeling. She is leveling with her husband, being honest about her negative feelings, but in a nonjudgmental way.

Evaluative, judgmental leveling would go something like this: "John, you never pay any attention to me at all. You are only concerned about yourself and what you want to do. You're more interested in the paper than you are in me. I wish you would quit being so inconsiderate and selfish and think of someone else just once." John is evaluated negatively as selfish, inconsiderate, and never paying attention to his wife. Obviously, he is going to defend himself against these judgments in some way, and her leveling attempt may lead to greater disruption or perhaps to a reluctant and uneasy modification of John's

80

behavior just to placate her.

Leveling comes from the other dimensions of the trusting relationship: from a sense of concern for another person, we let him know how we feel about his behavior. This is vital, for, if the person feels that leveling is motivated by revenge or a wish to punish rather than by concern and acceptance, it is likely to lead to a disruption of the relationship rather than to enhanced trust.

Family status often affects leveling. Father and mother, with the highest status, often are quite free to level with their children, but the children are not allowed to give them the same honest reactions. At its best, leveling is a two-way communication process. Parents need to know how their child responds to their behavior just as the child needs to know his parents' reaction to him. Also, leveling involves both positive and negative reactions. It is important for family members to know when they are liked and appreciated, in addition to finding out those things they do that elicit negative responses.

Trust is enhanced in the family if each family member can count on a high degree of openness from everyone else. Each can be "trusted" to let others know what he is thinking — to share deeply with the family — and each can trust the others to let him know, in a spirit of helpfulness, when he is engaging in behaviors that create problems for them — or for someone else. In addition, each knows when he is liked and appreciated. It is difficult to trust a person when you don't know where you stand with him; just as it is difficult to trust a person deeply who will not let you know what's bothering him or what his real concerns are. Openness is therefore an essential part of trust.

Integrity, caring, sharing, leveling — wisely and lovingly blended — contribute to the building of a trusting relationship.

11

SHARE

A cause of distress in many families is the change in the flow of information that occurs between spouses, between parents and children, and between brothers and sisters. When children are young they come to parents with everything — all the hurts, quarrels, concerns, fears, and joys of the day come pouring out like a full, gushing river. As they grow older, the stream seems to diminish slowly until there is only a trickle of sharing.

The same pattern sometimes develops between a husband and wife. Their marriage may start with a spontaneous exchange of all feelings, activities, and events, but time and circumstances often change the opportunity for, availability of, or interest in a continuation of this sharing with each other — often to the distress of both partners.

The Johari Window

Joseph Luft (with Harry Ingham) developed a model for depicting the pattern of communications between two (or more) people. Because it resembles the panes of a window, Luft and Ingham combined their two given names and called their model the Johari window. Figure 1 shows their basic model.

Quadrant 1 represents the arena of open communications — ideas, events, attitudes, feelings that both know about and feel free to discuss. There are things that both know about but deliberately do not mention, such as a painful fight or distressing situation; so there are some areas unavailable even in this quadrant, but generally we are looking at the shared aspects of a relationship.

Quadrant 2 indicates the area of data known to the self but unknown to the other (or others). One may keep hidden from others his true feelings, his ideas, his creative actions, his warmth, his experiences. There may be something in the relationship or the situation that keeps information from being shifted into Q1. Children often hide their actions from parents because of fear of what might happen if parents knew.

The third quadrant (Q3) represents the other side of the coin from Q2. An individual may find that others keep a great many things hidden. He is blind to their feelings about him, as well as to much about their backgrounds, experiences, attitudes, and feelings. Q3 represents all that others know about themselves but do not share with him.

Finally, quadrant 4 (Q4) is the hidden or unknown part of the relationship. Everyone has feelings, attitudes, or resources that he keeps repressed from himself and others, perhaps a rich area of potential that is yet untapped. For example, a man might have deep fears about becoming too close to anyone, fears he has kept so well hidden from himself and from others that they don't emerge into Q1 until he is married and suddenly feels threatened.

A more positive example of Q4 would be a girl, an only child, who has never been around children but who finds with the birth of her own a great capacity within herself for loving and caring for children, a potential waiting to be released.

A New Relationship

When two people begin a new relationship, the amount

84

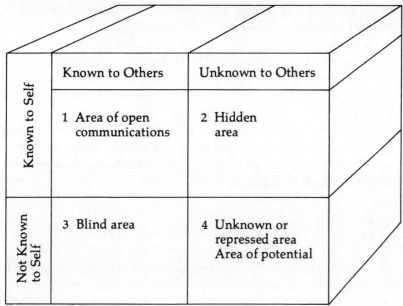

Figure 1: Johari window

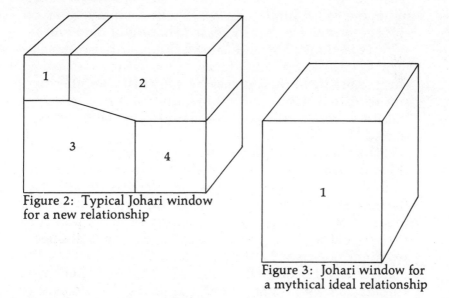

Figure 2: Typical Johari window
for a new relationship

Figure 3: Johari window for
a mythical ideal relationship

of shared data is small, Q2 and Q3 are larger, and Q4 is probably fairly constant. The resulting window might look like figure 2.

If appropriate opportunity, interest, and need evolve, the partners in the interaction will begin to shift data from Q2, 3, and 4 into Q1, which will begin to enlarge. Enlargement comes only as people feel safe, trustful, concerned, involved with each other. They must first feel that there is some "pay-off" for putting more of themselves, their feelings, ideas, and experiences, into the hopper for shared discussion.

The Trust Limit

There seems to develop in almost every relationship a trust limit — that point where one person begins to feel uneasy about sharing anything more with another. Sometimes the trust limit is self-imposed — one begins to feel uneasy or fearful about sharing for some personal reasons. Or it may be that the other person will determine the trust limit. He may, unknowingly, give off signals to indicate that increased sharing of data will result in reactions of censure, hurt feelings, criticism, resentment, ridicule, or indifference. One is not inclined to share more of himself unless he can trust the other person to listen, try to understand, and continue to accept him as a worthwhile person regardless of the data being shared.

It has been my own observation that in most relationships the trust limit is more restrictive than would be desirable for a fully satisfying and effective relationship. Barriers have been created to stop the flow of significant inputs that could be helpful in solving sensitive problems that cry out for solution. A challenge for most families is to extend the trust limit and expand Q1 until all needful matters can be considered and handled. The chapter on trust examines in more detail the forces that expand or reduce the limits of trust.

The Ideal Window

Some have asked, "What would the ideal Johari window look like, indicating that a family was fully effective?" It has been hypothesized that the ideal relationship would be like figure 3.

This model would assume that everything is shared with everyone else, that nothing is held back, and that all things are available to everyone. No one would have private thoughts or feelings, and there would be no holding back of thoughts, feelings, or actions that might wound or offend. Such a relationship, while being "ideally" open, might not be ideal in allowing for the optimum growth and enhancement of other aspects of the human personality.

Any ideal relationship depends on the goals of the persons involved, their level of experience and sensitivity, and the complexity of the situation which surrounds the relationship. What might be ideal for one family might be too limited or too open for another.

Experience has indicated certain propositions about the degree of openness in a relationship:

1. Most relationships are more restrictive than would be optimally healthy for all concerned.

2. There are some areas of privacy that should be held inviolate for all persons. Each should have the right to private thought, personal reflection or struggle, or unshared experience that in his judgment, if shared, would do nothing to enhance the relationship. (This proposition requires sensitive use, or it can be a justification for a great deal of nonsharing.)

3. There is a certain reciprocity in openness. People will share to the degree that others have shared with them. The problem occurs when everyone waits for someone else to begin.

4. Many of the barriers to sharing are self-imposed. The realities of what might happen if we share certain thoughts, feelings, or experiences are not nearly so dreadful as the results we imagine.

87

5. Q1 will expand primarily as Q2 and 3 diminish. People will need to begin to share more, elicit feedback from others, risk more, and ask for more than they have been used to doing.

6. Sound decisions are based on the degree of good information available. People will make personal or collective decisions differently depending on the amount of information available. If possible, all relevant data should be available before decisions are made.

7. Many families do not take the time or create the conditions that would allow data to be shared easily and without threat.

Opening the Window

The following conversation shows how to encourage openness among family members:

"John, I've noticed that you've been rather quiet and withdrawn for the past several days. You act worried, and it's not like you. Is there anything wrong that you would like to talk over with me?"

"Yeah, there are some things, Dad, but I think I need to work them out for myself."

"I'm not going to pry, John. I respect your right to personal privacy, but sometimes it helps to have someone else listen and get a different perspective on things. I think you can trust me to try to be honestly understanding and helpful."

"I know that, Dad, but I'm not sure that anyone can do anything but me."

"Often that's the case, and if you share your concern with me, and I feel that you have to handle this on your own, I'll tell you that straight from the shoulder."

"Well, it's like this, Dad. You know that Connie and I have been going together for quite awhile, and now she's getting pretty serious. I'm not sure what to do. . . ."

This father has helped his son "open the window." If we always wait for someone else to put data into Q1, it might take too long. The self-imposed barriers to sharing might be too strong, and help is needed to get concerns out in the open for healthy discussion.

Sharing — A Family Exercise

Have each member of your family rate himself in the following ways:

	Always	Sometimes	Never
1. As a family, we get together and make important plans and decisions.	_____	_____	_____
2. As a child, I feel free to talk over *serious* concerns with my dad.	_____	_____	_____
3. As a child, I feel free to talk over *serious* concerns with my mother.	_____	_____	_____
4. As a mother or father, I feel I can talk over important issues with the children.	_____	_____	_____
5. As a husband or wife, I feel a certain restriction or constraint in talking over important things with my spouse.	_____	_____	_____
6. Brothers and sisters in our family really talk to each other.	_____	_____	_____
7. We all like to sit and talk at the dinner table or in the front room.	_____	_____	_____
8. We find time for private talks between a parent and each child.	_____	_____	_____
9. I usually plan very carefully before I will discuss anything of real importance with anyone in the family.	_____	_____	_____
10. I often wish that our family would share more with each other.	_____	_____	_____

As you look at your responses to the statements, you will become more aware of the degree of openness or closedness of the sharing in your family. Is the sharing closed to everyone or to just one or two? Do others know how you feel and what you would really prefer your relationship to be?

Sharing begins with someone's being willing to take a little bit from Q2 and put it into the area of shared information. There are risks as well as rewards to sharing. Look at the Risks vs. Rewards table to see if the rewards outweigh the risks. If they do, sharing may be worth the risk.

Risks vs. Rewards in Sharing

Risk	Reward
1. If I share my problems, others may think I am dumb or stupid for having such problems.	1. If I share, others may understand and help me deal with my problems.
2. If I share, others may get angry or offended.	2. If I can share sincerely, others may appreciate what I say and we'll get closer together.
3. If I share, I may get hurt or rejected.	3. If I share, I may get greater acceptance.
4. If I share, I may be putting my burden on others.	4. If I share, others may be willing to share their burdens with me; maybe we can carry them together.

12

HELP

"I was only trying to be helpful" is the plaintive cry of many a parent who sees a child storm out of the house in a fit of resentment and rebellion. Being helped is always in the eyes of the helpee, not the one offering the help; or, stated another way, the intention to be helpful is not enough. Help must be experienced as such by the one to whom it is proffered — or it is really not help. In the best sense it is aiding another person to cope more adequately with conditions in his world.

Asking for Help

There are two major conditions that result in one person's giving help to another. One comes when one person goes to another and says something like this: "Have you got a minute? I'd like to talk to you about a problem." The request is initiated by the person needing help, and when it comes from child to parent, from husband to wife, or vice-versa, it makes extending assistance much easier.

For many people, asking for help is very difficult. It implies a lack of capability on their part to deal with their own situation. They may feel "one down" to the person being asked — in a kind of inferior position. Or they may prefer to be asked for help because it makes them feel needed and even superior. For whatever reason there are

91

those who hesitate or even refuse to ask for help from any-one even if they need it.

Offering to Help

The above attitude leads to the second, more difficult, condition for giving help — namely, offering it to some-one who hasn't asked.

Tom Jackson can see that his seventeen-year-old daugh-ter, Karen, is troubled. For several days she has been with-drawn, pale, restless, and irritable with other family mem-bers. All this is at variance with her generally easy-going, stable disposition. Tom wishes she could crawl into his lap and tell him her troubles the way she did as a child. Then he could comfort her, kiss away the fears, or apply a Band-Aid to the hurt. Now there seems to be a clear, unwritten sign which says, "Hands off. Leave me alone."

Karen feels alone, worried, and full of need. She and Mike have been going together for almost two years. Lately the physical attraction has become harder and harder to control, and she is afraid of what might happen. Breaking up with Mike would probably be best, but there was such an empty feeling when she thought of not being with him again. Her parents are concerned about her, she can tell. They make comments such as, "You don't seem to be your-self these days. Is anything the matter?" But how do you talk about such things? It would embarrass both them and her, she is sure.

One night she has just climbed in bed and turned off the light when her father comes quietly into her room and sits down beside her in the dark. "Karen, let me tell you a little about me. I remember when I had just graduated from high school, and my parents were all excited about my going to college. Every summer I had worked, and I had saved over a thousand dollars. I knew everyone expected me to go to college, and I'd always been an obedient boy — did what my folks wanted. But I had always wanted to get away on my own. I would daydream about getting a motorcycle and traveling around the country, or taking a tramp steamer to Europe and then walking and hitchhiking through interest-ing countries. I never told anyone about those feelings. Finally I went on to college the way I was expected to do. But I've often wished I had someone then to talk to, some-one who would have understood. We all need to be understood. Do you know what I'm trying to tell you, my precious daughter?"

"Yes, Daddy." And slowly the aching problem comes out.

When people don't ask for help, it does not mean they don't want it — or need it. Karen both wants and needs help. She does not know how to approach her parents, for she feels they (1) might not understand, (2) might judge or evaluate her negatively for having that particular problem, (3) might get angry or upset, or (4) might not have any real help with a solution.

I have given the story a positive ending, as the father and daughter begin to talk together. However, it is just as possible that even when the father has been sensitive in initiating help, the daughter might not accept the offer. Karen could have said, "Dad, I appreciate what you are trying to do, but this is something I just have to work out myself." The father's "help" would have already been given. He might not have helped by giving counsel or looking at alternative courses of action, but he helped by giving support, empathy, and understanding. This may be more important help than advice giving, and an unwise father may not understand that and feel a failure when actually he was a success.

Motives and Strategies

Any person who seeks to give help would be wise to examine his own motives. Giving help can be a seductive process, leading him to offer assistance more to meet his own needs than to satisfy those of the other person. Without being aware of it, a parent could be led into giving help to a child to relieve his own anxiety, to keep the child dependent, to feel wanted and needed, to feel important, or to display his experience or wisdom. While there is probably no such thing as purely unselfish behavior (we probably find some satisfaction in the most sincerely altruistic actions), behaviors that have a surface form of

93

unselfishness but at a deeper level are very personally motivated may result in more hurt than help. The parent who wants to help out of a desire to dominate or control or to show his expertise or authority will probably engage in actions that fulfill his needs more than they aid the child. A person is helped only if his ability to cope with the problem at hand is enhanced. What kinds of problem situations cause people to ask for or to respond with help?

1. Some need help to handle pain, loss, or sorrow.

2. Some need assistance in making decisions or finding solutions to problems.

3. Some need help in coping with an emotional state of anger, frustration, confusion, bitterness, or disappointment.

4. Some may need help in dealing with a problem person or situation.

5. Some may actually need a "helping hand" — direct, immediate work, muscle, or brain power — to keep from being overwhelmed.

Such a variety of needs requires a would-be helper to have at his disposal a variety of modes of action so that the other person will feel that he was helped. There are those who have only one strategy for giving assistance to others. Most common of these approaches is advice giving, usually couched in the phrase "If I were you, this is what I would do." It must always be remembered that what one person might do — given his personality, experience, and resources — may not be possible for another who has a different composite of resources.

Eric Berne describes different kinds of "games people play," and one of these revolves around advice giving and its rejection. The advice giver or suggestor keeps saying, "Why don't you try this?" or "If I were you I'd do this." And the helpee keeps saying, "I tried that and it didn't work," or "I couldn't do that in this situation," or something else that deflects or rejects the suggestions or advice. When such a game is played out, it usually means the person who asked for help really didn't want it in the form of advice. He needed something more or different, but the helper was locked into his single strategy and the "game" resulted.

Action, Not Asking

Most people want to be helpful to certain special others and usually want to appear helpful to most others. Certainly parents desire, almost always, to be of assistance to their children. When we pick up signals that another person needs some type of help, the most common initial reaction is to ask, "What can I do to help?" or "If you need anything, please let me know." For many people, to tell someone else what they need smacks of begging, and their pride resists that. The parent who has a suspicion that a child is lonely and needs some company or some involving activities can ask, "What's the matter, Son? Is there something I can do to help?" But he will often hear, "Oh, it's nothing." He might get a quite different response if he were to say, "Son, let's go bowling. I need some exercise. And why don't you call Bob and see if he would like to go with us?"

This is a sensitive point. To overplan or to organize too much may be seen as an intrusion and not as help, but most often the person who will take action that is on target with the situation will be more helpful and will be more appreciated than the one who is always asking how or whether he can help.

When to Deny Requests

It is a wise parent who knows enough about the needs of the children to know when not doing something or denying a request is more helpful in the long run than carrying out immediately what a child asks for.

Kent approaches his mother with a troubled look but a clear request. "Mom, the guys are all going to take shotguns and sleep out and then go rabbit hunting early in the morning. Can I go with them?"

95

Mrs. Hansen knows some things about her son. She is aware that he doesn't really like guns or killing animals but that the respect of his friends is very important. She suspects that Kent is feeling pressure to go hunting and to turn that down would be hard on a fourteen-year-old. So she says, "Kent, I don't think you ought to go. You have never passed the gun safety course, and there are a number of things that I need you to do for me tomorrow. I think you should tell your friends that you are sorry, but your mother wants you to stay home and do your work here. If you really decide another time to hunt, then you should plan ahead, pass the gun course, and be prepared."

She thinks she sees a look of relief on Kent's face as he goes to the phone to complain that his mother won't let him go.

All too often parents who try to be helpful wind up as servants to the desires and even to the whims of their children. At that point, being "helpful" ceases to do the child any good. A slavish doing for him does not ultimately help him to handle his world more effectively. It may do just the opposite. Sometimes parents can be most helpful when they say, "No, I won't do it. You'll have to do it yourself."

It would be best if parents, before they rush in to help in the guise of wanting to assist a child, would ask themselves honestly, "Am I doing this for him or for myself?" They might find that they bask in the reflected glory of the achievements of their children and that their assistance is a way of getting more achievement from the child so their own egos can be fed. Remember: Help is the giving of assistance that allows someone else to cope more effectively with his world.

13
DISCIPLINE

Too many parents deal with the matter of discipline by initially asking the wrong question. They ask, "How should I discipline my children?" It would seem wiser to query, "How can I help build discipline into my children?" The first question leads one to examine his behavior toward his children, and the second focuses on the end result one wishes to achieve.

The root word is *disciple* — connoting that one is dedicated to some goal, person, or value. How can one help a child become a disciple — a person who lives with dedication, in contrast to the person whose life is selfish, hedonistic, or willy-nilly? The foundation is a commitment to a set of values by the parents. They are, whether they like it or not, significant role models for their children, and each child will be influenced by the discipline displayed by them.

Because of commitment to a set of values, certain expectations develop within the family system. There are some things we do or do not do that are "expected" because "this is what we are in our family." For many years San Francisco's Chinatown has been a rock of family stability in a sea of delinquency and discord. Observers are impressed with the perpetuation of the old Chinese value of filial piety — parental respect. It is expected that children will pay respect to parents and others who are older. Parents comply with the same set of expectations, and children see the model well enacted by parents. Children are expected to behave in certain kinds of ways from the beginning, and consequently they do so.

Freedom of Choice

There are many parents who feel that they should not impose their value systems upon their children, that each child should be free to decide on his own what direction his life should take. Children do not wait until they are older, wiser, and more mature to develop a set of values and goal orientations. If the parents leave a vacuum in the value-goal area, the void will soon be filled by other adult models, peers, or influences via mass media. An investigation at Stanford of families with children who were drug users compared to families with children who were non-drug users is enlightening. Parents of drug users often took the position early in the lives of their children that they would not impose values but would let each child be free to "do his own thing," develop his own creative potential, and share in a close, easy-going relationship with his parents. As the children grew older, they adopted behaviors and practices with which the parents did not agree and which led to a disrupted relationship. The drug-using children were more conforming to the values of their peer group and less creative than were the non-drug-using children who had initially been exposed to strong traditional values through their parents.

The notion of anyone's having "pure," free choice uncontaminated by socialization, culture, and social influences is probably a myth. Parents are the most responsible socializing agents and probably help their children most by thinking through their own values and then representing them well. Parents who are not clear as to their own value positions or who declare values in marked contrast to their behavior create in their children either uncertainty or disillusionment. The children see what to

98

them is hypocritical behavior as parents mouth a belief that their actions belie.

Understanding Behavior

After reading this discussion to this point, some might say, "You're avoiding the issue. What do you do when your child disobeys, when he violates an agreement or understanding you have? Don't you 'discipline' the child, as the word commonly implies?"

Before discipline (in the sense of punishment or correction) should be applied, it is well to try to understand the supposedly deviant behavior from the perspective of the offender. Parents might well explore with the child the question "What led you to do what you did?" But they should realize that the child may not be able to give a clear, understandable explanation. The following story illustrates the polarity between a child's point of view and that of an adult:

> On his way to Sunday School, the ten-year-old boy with the slicked-down hair, scrubbed freckled face, and Sunday best comes upon a remarkable thing. Lying beside the path to the church house is a perfect stone. He picks it up and hefts it between his fingers. The weight is exactly right. It is just rough enough to grasp but smooth enough to let fly with ease. It is a stone made for throwing. Only once in a great while do you even find a stone that absolutely demands to be thrown with skill and rigor, and the target must be just right for such a rock. It must be a target far enough away to be a challenge, but close enough to promise success. "Maybe I'd better put this stone in my pocket until after Sunday School," thinks the boy. "But no. Suppose the teacher sees it and takes it away. What a terrible loss."
>
> Thinking such thoughts as he walks along, the boy suddenly sees the exact target for his perfect stone. Standing in front of the church house is the target meant to be mastered. It is a slim birch tree with a white, inviting trunk. Such a tree should be hit by this stone in his hand before anyone can disrupt this act of destiny. Taking careful aim, the boy throws his perfect stone with all his might.
>
> His aim is just off, perhaps because of his unaccustomed Sunday dress, and the beautiful stone crashes through the

front window of the chapel. The boy trembles with anguish. Should he run? No, he had better face the consequences like a man. He stands waiting while the red-faced, angry minister runs to his side. "Why did you do such a thing?" shouts the pastor.

"I don't know," replies the boy. How does a ten-year-old put into words the demand of the perfect stone to be thrown at exactly the right target?

It is possible that many things that are interpreted as disobedience might be understood in a different light if adults could only see things in the perspective of the child accused as disobedient. Perhaps parents should take the time and make the effort to see through the eyes of their children, as well as of others with whom they interact.

Expressing Feelings

At times children do engage in behaviors that violate understood and hopefully accepted family standards and values expressed by parents. The reaction of parents at such times is usually a feeling of hurt, anger, or resentment. Some parents are inclined to "act out" these feelings by spanking, slapping, verbal abuse, or the imposition of some form of restriction, fine, or punishment. Perhaps the starting place should be an expression of feelings and not the acted-out punishment. Consider the following incident:

It is after 2:30 a.m., and Marsha is not home yet. Both her mother and father are awake, filled with worry and concern. It was agreed that Marsha, who was sixteen and just starting to date, would be in between 12:30 and 1:00 a.m. She is usually so dependable that her parents feel something must have happened to keep her out so late. Should they call the boy's home, the police?

Then they hear the sound of a car in the driveway. In a moment Marsha slips in the back door. She looks guilty and sheepish when she sees her parents waiting for her. "Where have you been?" both parents ask together.

Marsha explains, "After the dance a group of us went over to Janet's house to listen to records and have something to eat, and I just lost track of the time."

"Couldn't you have called us?" asks her father.

"I could have," says Marsha, "but I just forgot to look at the time, and then I left when I saw it was so late."

Father looks steadily at his daughter and says slowly, "Marsha, I can understand how it is possible to get involved and lose track of time. But you should also know that because you did you left your mother and me waiting here imagining all kinds of things that might have happened to you. Right now I'm glad you're home, but I'm also angry and upset with you because you were not more responsible. We had an agreement that you would be in by 1:00. When our agreements are violated, I am going to have some strong emotional reactions. You need to know that. I'll be fair in making agreements with you, but you must be responsible in keeping them."

This father has expressed clearly his anger and his concern. He has also referred to agreements made with his daughter. If she can behave so as to be consistent with agreements she has made of her own volition, she has entered into the world of self-discipline.

Making Agreements

An important process in building discipline is the reaching of agreements. They may be reached by the whole family and expected of all: for example, all agree to make their beds, keep their rooms picked up, take turns with the supper dishes, go to school on time, and come straight home. Or they may be made specifically with each child, such as "You may have the car two nights a week." Each agreement should include a clear understanding of what is expected and what the consequences will be both of fulfilling the agreement and of violating it. Agreements are personal contracts entered into by choice and are based on a clear understanding of all the issues involved. An imposed rule is not an agreement. There may be occasions when parents feel they must impose a rule, but usually agreements will achieve more discipline in the child. Agreements fail when parents will not take the time to manage an agreement system. An agreement is based on:

101

1. A clear understanding of the issues involved.

2. A clarification of the expectations on both sides — what does each expect of the other in terms of how and when the agreement should be carried out?

3. Decisions about consequences — what will happen if the agreement is violated?

4. Consistency in following through after the agreement is reached.

Many families who try agreements fail because (1) the children feel "forced" into the agreement, (2) certain aspects of the agreement have not been clarified, or (3) parents collapse in following through on appropriate consequences.

What are some of the consequences? Parents should reinforce all the good behaviors they want to support and encourage in their children. It is good to praise, recognize, or give a gift or allowance for agreements met or exceeded. It is also appropriate to become angry, to share feelings, and to deny or restrict certain privileges when the restrictions have been accepted as part of the agreement system.

Agreements often need refining and modifying as time goes on. One appropriate for a twelve-year-old may not be adequate when that same child is fifteen.

Applying the "Increase of Love" Principle

Remember, the end result of all "disciplining" is to build discipline *into* the child. There is strong evidence that discipline that flows out of love and understanding and an agreement system that is fair and "makes sense" have a good chance of succeeding.

When a serious violation occurs, as they sometimes do, and the full measure of anger and restriction is meted out, it is vital that the child (of any age) be assured that he is loved and accepted although certain of his actions are not. This important principle — to extend an even greater amount of love toward the person who has just been chastised so he will know that he is a person of worth who

is still loved even though his actions have been rejected —
is neglected by many parents. Some seem to take per-
verse delight in continuing to punish the child long after
the incident should have been resolved and forgotten.

Building discipline into children takes time; imposing
discipline does not — immediately. But the long-range
consequences of seeing a child live a life of discipline because he has lived with parents who had clear values, who
tried to understand and be fair, and who took time to
manage a just discipline system is well worth the effort
involved.

14

DON'T
BE TOO BUSY

The headline of a magazine article highlights an apparent disease of our modern society: "Parents Too Busy." According to this and many other stories, today's parents are so involved in work, clubs, social activities, bridge parties, and/or seeking after material gain that they don't have time to spend talking with their children. The burden of the problems of modern young people is placed squarely in the laps of the parents. However, in the language of today, to place the blame on parents for the failures of the children may be a "cop-out."

Certainly there are parents whose lives are so involved with other things that they do not spend time with their children. But the opposite is also true. There are many children, particularly teenagers, who are so busy, so involved in the demands of their world, that they do not have time for their parents. In these cases it is the child — not the parent — who is "too busy" to spend time building the family.

It is not uncommon to find the modern teenager with a daily schedule that looks something like this:

7:00 a.m.	Get up, get ready for the day, and eat something for breakfast.
8:00 a.m.	Classes begin at school.
3:00 p.m.	Classes end.

3:00–6:00 p.m.	Athletics, drama, music, debate, drill teams or work part-time or get together with friends.
6:00–7:00 p.m.	Eat supper. Maybe help with the dishes.
7:30–9:30 p.m.	Study or talk on the phone to friends or get together with friends to plan an activity or "goof off."
10:00–11:00 p.m.	Sometime in here get things finished and flop into bed.

Typical Family Discussions

In this hectic pace, parents frequently find themselves trying to catch their son or daughter for a few minutes of visiting. The dinner table is often the only place where most of the family is together during the day, and a common scene at the table is to watch mother or dad trying to pump out a little information from their frantically scheduled offspring.

> Mother: "How did things go at school today, Jim?"
> Jim: "OK."
> Dad: "Anything interesting happen?"
> Jim: "Nope."
> Mother: "How did your math class go? I know you've been worried about it."
> Jim: "It's going all right."
> Dad: "How is your men's chorus doing?"
> Jim: "Good."
> Dad: "Any problems coming up that we can help with?"
> Jim: "Not really, but can I have the car tonight? I need to get together with some of the kids."
> Dad: "I guess so."

In fairness to the teenagers, it is not just from them that parents try to "pump" information. If you were to listen to the conversation between a mother and dad when he came home from work, you would probably have heard a conversation like this:

> Mother: "How did things go at work today, dear?"
> Dad: "OK."

106

Mother: "Anything interesting happen?"
Dad: "Nope."
Mother: "How did that new project go that you've been worried about?"
Dad: "It's going all right."

Family members often don't spend much time talking, sharing, discussing. We find few times when everyone is there, and the climate for discussion is not created since everyone is rushing through dinner to get to the next activity. The lack of scheduling of family time is just as much a problem for the children as for the parents. Younger children often are the ones that suffer. They would like to get together with the whole family more — to play games and do things together. Many teenagers don't really know anything about their younger brothers or sisters. The "small fry" live in a world of their own, and the teenager only occasionally dips into that world. It is often a surprise to the teenager to find that a younger brother or sister has grown up or has developed habits or attitudes he can't understand. Older brothers and sisters are important role models and sources of influence on younger children. What a loss it is when the older children are too involved to exert the right kind of influence on younger children! What a loss of potentially powerful example!

Lip-service Priorities

If you were to ask most teenagers what is most important to them, most would answer, "My family." If you were to examine where they actually spend their time, their actions (and often their parents' actions) belie their words. People of all ages have lip-service priorities — they say some things are important but spend their time on things they would say have much lower priority. It is a real dilemma for the young person because a lower-priority activity, like athletics or doing things with friends, has a great deal of immediate reward and satisfaction. One gets more fun, acceptance, status, and ex-

107

I'm worried about
what I'm going to do
after I graduate and
I wish I had more friends.
What can I do about it?

citement right now from the lower-priority situations, and it is hard to withdraw from them.

How to Fulfill our Major Goals

Perhaps with better planning and some willingness to sacrifice immediate pleasures it might be possible to meet more of our own top-priority goals.

Start with Positive Assumptions

Much of the action we take begins with the assumptions we make. If we assume that the PTA meeting is going to be boring, we probably won't go; or if we do, we act in a lackadaisical fashion so we make our assumptions come true. We don't have a good time because we behave in such a way and with such an attitude that we could not possibly have a good time.

The same thing is true at home. If you (son or daughter) assume that Mother and Dad are too busy, they don't understand, or they aren't interested, then you don't talk with them about anything of importance. Let me suggest another set of assumptions:

Assume that your parents love you, are vitally concerned about your happiness, and would prefer to connect with you in a meaningful way above anything else they could do.

Also assume that your parents are a little timid about trying to get into your life and probably have limited skills in how to open up a real discussion with you. If you can make these positive assumptions, then perhaps you can take the next step.

Take a Risk

Young people today are often pictured as high risk takers. They are seen as wanting lots of speed, new adventures, new excitements. This may be true in some areas, but in the human relations area, particularly in the family, there are too many nonriskers — people who prefer to play it safe.

The risk in a relationship is to initiate — get something started. I would be willing to make a promise to any teenager. If you really want to have a significant discussion with your mother or dad, and if you will go and say the following to them, you will get positive results. You should say: "Mother (or Dad), I really would like to sit down and talk with you. I would like your advice. I need some help with something that concerns me."

The promise is that if you do this sincerely, your parent will make arrangements to talk with you and will be glad for the chance. What will you talk about? If you have a real problem, you deal with that. Examples:

> I'm worried about what I'm going to do after I graduate.
> I wish I had more friends. What can I do about it?
> How do I do a better job in my school (club or church) position?

If no problem comes immediately to mind, then deal with your relationship with that parent. Examples:

> Dad, I wish we were closer. What can I do to make it so we have more fun together?
> Mom, I know sometimes you get upset with me. How can we work it out so we make each other happier?

It is a risk to start talking. We risk the possibility of being misunderstood or rejected or laughed at, but by not taking the risk, we may give up the chance for warmth and closeness and satisfaction with a family that hopefully we can be with forever.

Starting to talk takes time. Someone has to start calling time out from the hectic schedules we have today. Parents would like to but often find their teenage children are too busy. Perhaps the teenagers need to examine themselves to see if the "too busy" sign is a problem they have — and need to solve.

15

DEAL
WITH THREAT

Abraham Maslow, the late pioneer in humanistic psychology, identified what he felt were the basic needs of all human beings. The lowest and most primitive were biological and safety needs — food, water, air, and freedom from physical danger. Then came social needs — to be included and to like and be liked by others. At the next level were ego needs — to be thought well of, to be esteemed by others, to feel worthwhile. Finally, according to Maslow, if these prior needs could be met, it might be possible for a person to reach out and to "actualize" himself — to become his best self and thus fulfill his self-actualizing capabilities.

If Maslow is correct, all of us are motivated by these needs, and anything that thwarts, diminishes, or disrupts one or more of them will be seen as a threat. When we are threatened, the prediction is that we will respond in some way that will protect us from the potential disturbing influence.

Since the home is the place where all these basic needs receive primary attention, it is apparent that the greatest potential threat lurks within the family system. Here is the possibility for greatest need satisfaction and also for greatest need disruption.

111

What Threatens People?

If we think of threat as any action, situation, or person capable of thwarting an important human need or actually or potentially causing a person to feel less adequate, less secure, less capable than he would like, the list of things that could possibly threaten each of us becomes almost endless.

In a family many subtle things can be threatening and may or may not be recognized or admitted. The following list of potential threats to various needs is not definitive but offers a few suggestions:

Needs	*Possible Threats in the Family*
1. Self-actualization	1. Denying someone an opportunity for a new growth experience
	2. Forcing someone to keep doing things the same way without good reason
2. Ego	1. Rejecting someone's ideas or suggestions
	2. Putting someone down — evaluative feedback or ego-deflating criticism
	3. Causing someone embarrassment by unusual appearance or actions
3. Social	1. Avoiding someone
	2. Not including someone in the family in a social activity
	3. Not allowing someone to behave so that his friends or peer group would approve
4. Safety	1. Physical punishment or promise thereof
	2. Leaving children alone or unattended
	3. Withdrawal of love or appearance thereof

| 5. Biological | 1. Loss of income for basic commodities |
| | 2. Denying a basic physical resource — food, rest, shelter, medical care |

One does not have to be consciously involved to be a threat to another family member. If a boy's sister or brother (or parents) behave publicly in a way that embarrasses him, it poses a threat to him. Since family members are usually seen as an extension of oneself, when the boy sees any of them behaving in a way that is unseemly to him, he feels personally diminished in terms of how he fears others are reacting. If his parents are not dressed correctly, try to join in with his friends, or just generally do not measure up to some standard (of which they may be totally unaware), they may cause a child at times to feel threatened.

Reactions to Threat

How can one tell if family members feel threatened? An English group therapist identified four common responses people make to feelings of threat. His formulation may help in identifying times when a threat exists in the family. If we see the signals, we may guess that some threat exists and try some type of remedial action, for if family members are expending time and energy to reduce the anxiety resulting from their fear of disruption, they are not using their personal resources for learning and growth.

1. Flight

A common response to threat is flight. When a person feels threatened, one way of reacting defensively is to withdraw or to run away. In the family if a child feels the possibility of being socially rejected or "put down" or laughed at by another family member, he may handle the situation by avoiding the person, clamming up and not saying anything, or staying away from home.

If a subject or an issue is threatening, we also engage in flight behavior by avoiding or dropping the subject if it ever comes up or is alluded to. Flight is a common defense against threat, and most people use it at one time or another. If it persists too long, it can be disruptive to the family relationship, for people do not get together. They avoid each other and issues that probably need to be handled or solved.

2. Fight

A second defense is fight behavior — a good offense is the best defense. When someone does something that makes a person feel less adequate, less secure, less accepted, he may respond by attacking. If a boy's older brother makes a disparaging remark about him, and if the boys are young, they may wind up in a physical fight. Later, the same type of remark may result in a verbal battle — arguing or bickering. Sometimes a person is so used to expecting a "put-down" or disparaging comment that he may react with a hostile defense even though the other person did not intend the remark the way it was heard.

Fight behavior can be transferred to someone who is less capable of defense than the person who actually poses the threat. A father may be very threatening to his children, and they are afraid to fight with him either physically or verbally, so they may take their feelings out in fight form on each other, the mother, the teacher, or friends. It is not uncommon for children to transfer the fight feelings generated against their parents to all authority persons, and they go through much of their lives fighting bosses, teachers, police.

3. Pairing

Another way people have of protecting themselves from threat is to pair up with one or two others — to get a friend for support. If the father is a source of threat in the family, a child may go to the mother for support, pair up with a brother or sister, or get together with a friend. In this pairing situation they can ventilate their feelings, feel support, escape into nonthreatening activities, or create fantasy reactions against the threat. Pairing can also be accompanied with flight — the pair go together as they avoid the threatening situation or escape from it.

When the threat comes from outside the home — from teachers, bullies, or situations (like not being accepted in a club or team) — family members may appropriately come to other family members and pair up to find the support and affection they need.

4. Dependency

The fourth defensive reaction is dependency. This represents a method of going to the source of threat and trying to reduce the fear by doing everything the threatening person or persons want of you. There is the subtle feeling that if one can always meet the other's expectations, do things just right, follow directions exactly, the result will always be reward or praise or acceptance from the threatening person, and one will then be safe or free from possible upset or disruption.

There are times when dependency can be an appropriate response; we can be legitimately dependent on someone who may pose a threat to us. People often fear the physician and try to alleviate their fear by doing exactly as he says.

However, persistent dependency may be crippling. As a child becomes dependent on his parents as a means of insuring approval, avoiding displeasure, and receiving constant support, he may find it difficult to break away and work either on his own or with someone else.

Coping with Threat

Should signs of threat reaction appear in a family, it is possible to do something about it — to try to reduce the threat or to manage it more appropriately.

Parents should realize that threat is probably mostly centered in them, and they may need to learn to use their power and authority in ways that do not result in negative reactions such as continual flight or escape from home, constant fighting, inappropriate pairing, or crippling dependency.

Sometimes a parent is not aware of his own threat potential, and a chance to get honest reactions from other family members may be of great value. (See the chapter on feedback.) Threat can be reduced if one or more of the following actions can be taken:

1. Problems of threat, fear, and/or anxiety can be discussed openly between family members.

2. Family members can experience the threatening person in new or different situations or under different conditions that are less threatening. A mother who is threatening because she is always punishing children for problems about chores or schoolwork may look for ways to relax, talk deeply, or recreate with her children.

3. Family members can engage in new and satisfying work or goal-accomplishment projects together.

4. The threatening person can help others to understand something of his needs, goals, background, experiences.

5. The person being threatened can tell the threatening person, "I've got a problem with you" — and they can try to work out a better solution to the problem.

6. An outsider can help family members explore their situation and find ways of relating with reduced threat.

The possibility of threat is always present in every family. If family members are sensitive and observant, they may pick up "threat signals" and begin to engage in more appropriate, threat-reducing actions.

16

USE FEEDBACK*

Interpersonal behavior usually begins with one person's initiation of action toward one or more others to achieve some purpose or goal. A parent, for example, may talk to a child to clarify a point, to give instructions, to stimulate, encourage, or support. If we were to diagram the interpersonal flow it would look like the figure on page 120.

Mr. Johnson has some *intention* toward his son, Tom. He wants to encourage, clarify, instruct, or to produce some result. Hopefully the impact he has on Tom will be consistent with his intentions. However, between *intention* and *impact* are two major gaps that must be considered and to some degree managed. Mr. Johnson must translate his intentions into behavior. For some people most of the time, and for others some of the time, this is a major difficulty. The behavior expressed may be a very clumsy representation of the intention. If you were to talk with the children of some parents, you would find they feel hostile, defensive, and resistant. A conversation with the parent would disclose that he is distressed that his children feel as they do, for he certainly did not intend that reaction.

Sometimes a person has unconscious intentions that are displayed exceptionally well. Mother may at some

*Revised. Reprinted by permission from the *Personnel Administrator*, "Encouraging feedback," June 1974.

deeper level distrust her children or husband, and her behavior communicates the message unmistakably. At the conscious level she would say that the communication of distrust is not her intention. Unless she can clearly understand her underlying intentions, she may continue to create problems she does not consciously want to have. One of the important reasons for feedback is to help the receiver examine, honestly, his total intention system, both conscious and unconscious.

However, the distortion between meaning and impact may be in the "eye of the beholder." Mr. Johnson's behavior may be a very clear representation of his intentions, but if Tom has a clogged filter system or perceptual screen and perceives the behavior quite differently than was intended, the resulting impact will not be what the father desires. Son Tom may have a thick anti-authority filter and resent anything any superior, particularly his father, does. He interprets attempts to clarify or encourage as disapproval or control. All of us have filters — some parts of which we are aware and others to which we are blind. Our filters are made up of our biases, prejudices, values, experiences, and feelings.

In either event, whether the problem of the undesirable impact results from gap 1 or gap 2, the result for the father is the same: he has not achieved the consequence he intended.

The Skill of Eliciting Feedback

In much of our current organization life, people have learned to mask, hide, and cover up their feelings, particularly those towards people in positions of power and influence. It is sometimes extremely difficult for a parent to know truly what his impact on others has been. He may see only the polite smile, the ready agreement, the apparent consensus and may assume, falsely, that the external feedback cues really represent the total impact.

The person with good interpersonal skills has ways of checking out data to determine his actual impact and to ascertain whether the problem, if any, is in his own inability to correctly communicate his conscious intentions or in the filter system of the other.

In training sessions with parents from many walks of life, I have asked, "Would you like to know the things you do that create problems for your children, or for your spouse?" Almost all indicated a desire to have such information.

When asked, "What is your current method for gathering such information?" fewer than 10 percent responded that they currently had a reliable, systematic strategy for gathering such data. Yet in the process of improving one's performance, probably no skill is more important than being able to gather accurate, honest feedback about one's impact on others.

In the past, much of the theory and research on feedback has centered on the method of giving such information. This is also an area of sensitive skill, for most people feel fearful and inept when it comes to sharing how they feel about someone's performance directly with him.

> Jack Douglas is an average teenager. He gets pretty good grades, plays intramural basketball, and is a clarinet player in the school band. His buddies are mostly a year older and like to cruise around in a car in the evenings. Jack doesn't see anything wrong with this as long as he keeps up with his schoolwork, but lately his dad has made life miserable for him. It seems to Jack that his dad is always on him about something or other — he can't ever seem to please him.
>
> One of his friends asks, "Jack, why don't you go and ask your dad what the matter is?"
>
> Jack's response is, "I don't think it would do any good. If I said anything, it would just make him mad, and he'd be more uptight than he is now."

If Jack were asked, "If your dad were to talk to you man to man and ask you how you felt about your relationship with him, would you be able to tell him how you feel?"

Jack might reply, "Well, if I felt he was really serious

The interpersonal flow

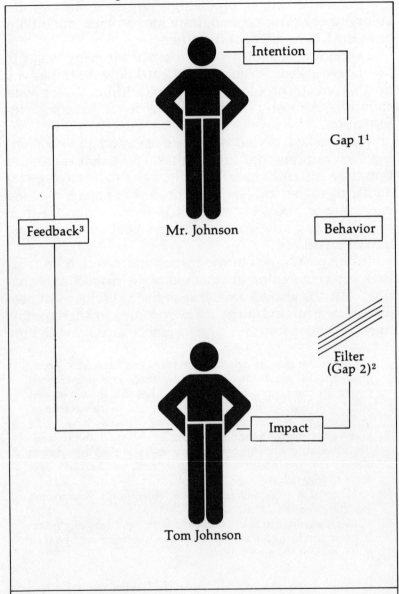

1. Gap 1 is the difference between one's intentions and the behavior that represents them.
2. Gap 2 is the difference between one person's behavior and the other person's perception of it.
3. Feedback is finding out how our behavior has been received by others.

in the request and would listen without getting too upset and defensive, I think I might share some of my reactions with him."

It is not easy for a person in a lower-status position in any organization to go to a more powerful, higher-status person and give feedback that is unsolicited and presumably unwanted. This is certainly true for many children where their parents are concerned. The risks involved are so great from the lower-status person's perspective that unless the situation becomes intolerable, or he is ready to quit, the safest course appears to be to remain silent, to "sweat it out," and to hope the passing of time will improve conditions.

This silent, sweat-it-out strategy has been observed in managers, college roommates, and married couples. It seems to be a widely utilized strategy for coping with people who have negative impacts on us. It is also a minimal change strategy that masks the real conditions and keeps frustration and negativism underground. Until reactions have surfaced, dealing with the negative consequences of a poor relationship is difficult.

However, if a parent were to initiate a process where he *asked* for the feedback and could set a climate where a child would feel safe or even rewarded for sharing information, then more children might be willing to share sensitive feedback. How do you go about eliciting feedback from others? Following are some suggested methods:

1. *Individual Direct Request*

Probably the simplest feedback-eliciting method is to invite another person to a private, one-to-one session. This could be preceded by a written note or verbal request stating the purpose of the visit and thus giving the person time to prepare. (Example: Dear Son: I would like very much to get your reactions about my behavior as your father. Do you see anything I do that creates problems for you or others in the family? Do you have any suggestions as to how I might improve my effectiveness? I'd like to get together and talk about this with you. Let's try to get together next Monday night about 9:30. Love, Dad.)

2. *Written Feedback*

A second method is to request (either verbally or by note) the person (or persons) to share his feedback in writing. (Example: Dear Sue: I'm honestly trying to become a more effective mother. Would you be willing to take some time out and write down any suggestions you have for my improvement? Try to be as honest as possible. I want the feedback, and feel it's important that I find out what the feelings of others in the family are, both positive and negative. If you would write them down and put your note on my bed sometime next week, I'd appreciate it. Love, Mother.)

It is apparent that, in the direct request for either verbal or written feedback, the person to whom the request is directed may feel "on the spot." If it is a parent making the request, a child may feel obligated to say something but be uneasy because of the risks involved. Direct request data are not anonymous, and he may wonder how direct he can be without creating problems. In order to stimulate the feedback, the following might be used:

3. *"Priming the Pump"*

This is a method of stimulating the flow of data by sharing some data already known. This process was observed in a training program where one participant was generating negative feelings in others. Every time a serious, deep, or sensitive discussion was underway, this man would sit with what was later described as a "snotty sneer" on his face. It was apparent that the other participants resented it, and rumblings were evident. The second day the man said to the group, "Whenever I get emotional or nervous, I know that my face twitches up. It's something I can't seem to control. Some people have said it looks like a 'snotty sneer.' Have you been aware of this?" This was a great releasing factor, and people

122

talked freely about their reactions to him. It was easy now for them to discuss his behavior since he had opened the subject and had some awareness of it. A parent could help release feedback in similar fashion. (Example: "Children, one of the things I think I do that upsets you is to react in a punishing way before you have a chance to explain. Are you aware of this?" Chorus: "Yeah. Right on, Dad."

4. Total Family Discussion

It is possible for a parent or child to use the whole family at a family meeting to discuss his behavior and to give him suggestions for improvement. To prepare the family, this issue could be part of the family agenda so that everyone would know it is going to be discussed at the next meeting. Such a meeting requires a general climate of openness, a spirit of dealing directly with sensitive issues in an atmosphere of concern and mutual help.

The format of the meeting could vary. The person wanting feedback could summarize his impressions of his own style and ask for reactions. He could ask each person to express his reactions and share his feedback and suggestions. The family could subgroup for a few minutes and then come back for a discussion all together.

5. Sharing One's Personal Assessment

This method is similar to the pump-priming process mentioned above. The person eliciting the feedback writes up an assessment of his own performance and asks others to confirm or deny his assessment, to share additional reactions, and to make any suggestions for improvement. (Example of written memo to family: I have written up the following assessment of my own performance as a parent. Would you indicate whether you agree or disagree with the various points, what your own reactions are, and any suggestions you have for improvement?)

My Assessment

As I see myself, I feel I do the following things well:

1. I think I am punctual and never miss appointments or keep people waiting.

2. I feel I am dependable in taking care of assignments or requests given to me.

3. I see myself as a hard-working person who has great dedication and loyalty to the family and its goals.

I also see the following critical things about my performance:

1. I feel that I am a rather closed person and that I don't communicate very much or very easily. I would like to improve this, but I'm not sure exactly how.

2. I think I tend to cut people off and am somewhat rejecting of new ideas. I'm not exactly sure how others see this or react to it.

3. I also think the children are a little afraid of me and feel a little uncomfortable talking with me. I don't know what gives them that impression or what I can do to reduce it.

Any additional reactions or suggestions:

124

6. Outside Assistance

Another method for gathering feedback data is to have an outside person assist. This person could be a minister, a friend, or a professional counselor. A variety of methods are available to him to gather feedback about a family member's performance. He may have already observed the person's behavior at other times. He can interview other family members and get their direct expressions. He can meet with the whole family for an open feedback session. The advantage of the outsider is that he can often see things to which insiders have become oblivious and can probe in areas sometimes not available to the person wanting feedback. A disadvantage is that the family may become dependent on the outsider and may never learn to give and receive helpful feedback as a regular part of their own ongoing relationship.

When You Receive Feedback

If a family member begins to elicit feedback, there are a few important guidelines regarding the manner of accepting the data. For most people sharing data with anyone is an especially high-risk activity. When it is first attempted, the sharer usually watches the other very closely to see how he reacts. This reaction usually determines whether such feedback will be given again or will be a one-time-only affair.

1. Listen, Don't Explain or Justify

There is a terrible tendency to want to explain or justify our actions when we receive feedback that we feel is unjustified or unwarranted or that stems from a misunderstood situation. When you ask for feedback, the burden is on you to *listen and try to understand.* This does not mean you are obliged to believe or accept the information, but your responsibility is to try to understand why the other person feels and reacts the way he does. Defensive behavior usually stifles the flow of feedback communications, for it tells the other person you are more interested in justifying yourself than understanding him.

2. Ask for More

Especially in the open, verbal feedback process there is an opportunity to get additional information. The first feedback that comes is usually guarded, cautious, and tentative. Depending on the reaction, the person giving the feedback will either be encouraged to continue, or he will close off the flow of information as being too risky or unproductive.

If the person eliciting the data can honestly keep saying, "That's extremely helpful and enlightening. Tell me more. Is there anything else I should know about that?" he will support and encourage a continuing flow of feedback.

3. Express an Honest Reaction

The person giving the feedback often wants to know what your reaction is to the data he has presented. The best guideline is to express your honest reaction. Examples of possible reactions follow:

> "That's really surprising to me. I didn't know you felt that way."

> "It shakes me up to hear that, but I think you've raised a most important issue."

> "I'm truly sorry to know that you've had those kinds of reactions. I hope I can do something about it."

> "I'm glad to get your reactions. That's different feedback from what I've received from others. I'd like to talk more about it."

4. Express Appreciation and Plan for the Future

If you elicit data and another person takes the time and risk to respond, your understanding and appreciation of his efforts should be expressed. This can be done by acknowledging the risk that probably was involved and sharing your appreciation for his efforts. At the same time, it is a good opportunity to plan ahead for future feedback sessions. The first session is usually the most difficult, and future sessions can be less disturbing and more productive. The purpose for starting the feedback process is to make it a regular part of the activity between you and others so you can continually learn from them. (Example: "Family, I want you to know I appreciate your feedback. I know it isn't easy to share reactions with others, and I have tried to listen and have found this very helpful to me. I hope we can do this again. Would you mind getting together in a few months for another discussion like this? I'll take the initiative to set up another session.")

After Feedback — What?

In terms of the initial model of human interaction (page 120), eliciting feedback helps a person determine whether the impact achieved is the one desired. If it is not, he still must ascertain whether the problem is in gap 1 or gap 2. If data have been gathered from several people and all are getting a similar reaction, it probably means that the behavior in gap 1 is causing the problem. At this point one is faced with the very difficult process — behavior change. It is not easy to begin to alter ways of functioning that have been established through the years. If one has had a style of being rather closed, rigid, authoritative and controlling, noncommunicative, or unorganized, it requires discipline and dedication to plan for change. Change is never easy.

Group Support

We might take a page from the book of some of the most successful change programs known — Alcoholics Anonymous, Synonon (Drug Addiction), and Weight

127

Watchers. Each uses the method of group support as an essential ingredient. The person desiring the change admits his problem and asks for others to support his change effort. A family member can initiate a similar process. By talking with those he has selected as support persons or with the whole family, he can identify his change goals, ask for suggestions for improvement, and request support and assistance as he works for improvement.

Continued Dialogue

If, however, the feedback seems to indicate the problem of negative impact is located in the other person's filter system, it indicates the necessity for continued dialogue with him. At this point the elicitor of feedback becomes the giver of feedback as he discusses with the other person issues about the latter's perception and filtering processes. The important factor is to *stay in dialogue*. If the first person is not getting the impact he desires and the problem is the perceiver, he needs to have wider dialogue, to share more of his intentions, to get more discussion faster about what he intends and what the other receives, and to try to go through a more rapid clarification. Too often it is easier to stop talking, avoid each other, assume it's "his problem," and thus leave a skeleton in the closet. If the interaction is significant enough and the results important enough, continued dialogue is not too great a price to pay.

AFTERWORD

So you have finished reading this volume. Any author has as a central query, "What did you think of my efforts? What are your reactions?" I am no exception. I wonder how you have felt about the ideas expressed, and I wonder most if anything you have read has had a strong enough impact to encourage you to take that first step toward creating your own closer family.

Perhaps as you have read the book you have seen mirrored in the writings a picture of some part of your own family. It should be comforting to know that your family is not entirely unique. All families have some problems — there is nothing wrong with that. The issue is this: Are you willing to try to make it better? Can you try again with greater insight, sensitivity, and skill? I hope so. One person has wisely said about family problems that the only time one has failed is after he has given up entirely.

As you have read this work, I am sure you have detected that I am a strong advocate of more and more family communications. Problems become compounded when people cease to talk about them in a positive, problem-solving way. Skeletons go into closets, inappropriate patterns become established, trips to Abilene are taken, when someone says to himself, "It's not worth it. I'm just going to keep my mouth shut." But there is the element of skill involved, too. More communications of the accusing, nagging, punishing variety may indeed not help. We need to start talking — taking risks — from a stance of truly caring about the other person and expressing that caring in word and action.

It is the nature of much human change that patterns alter slowly. Personalities, attitudes, feelings, and habits have been deeply formed and do not modify without effort. That is a great safeguard. If we all changed with every new input from any source, we would be like rudderless ships, driven by every wind and wave. Only those actions that are strong, consistent, rightly motivated, and persistent are likely to have an impact for positive change. Thus, change in a family must be seen as a long-range effort. You should not become too discouraged when improvements are achieved by gradual increments rather than by giant strides.

There is an old story of a group of village boys who decided that for once they would trick the local wise man into making a wrong judgment. One boy caught a bird and held it in his hand. He told the others, "When we go to the wise man, I will ask him what I have in my hand. Seeing the feathers, he will correctly say that I have a bird. Then I will ask, 'Is it dead or alive?' If he says it is alive, I will squeeze my fingers and crush the bird to death. Should he tell us that it is dead, I will open my hand and the bird will fly free. Either way, this time the wise man will be wrong."

The boys gathered at the wise man's home to carry out their plan. The leader held out his hand and asked, "Old man, what do I have in my hand?"

"You have a bird."

"Is the bird dead or alive?"

The old man looked the boy steadily in the eyes and responded, "My son, that is entirely up to you."

And so it is with all of us. What we do with our own insights or desires for improvement is entirely up to us — whether or not we will take the first steps for creating a closer family.

ABOUT
THE AUTHOR

William G. Dyer is a professor and past chairman of the Organizational Behavior Department at Brigham Young University — currently one of the top-ranked organizational behavior departments in the nation. He holds bachelor's and master's degrees in sociology from BYU and a doctorate in sociology from the University of Wisconsin. During the past twenty years, he has taught at the university level, held various administrative positions, and consulted with over thirty major business firms, church organizations, and government agencies. He has written six books (including *Insight to Impact: Strategies for Interpersonal and Organizational Change*, an organizational behavior text to be published in spring 1976 by Brigham Young University Press) and more than forty articles. His extensive background in employee- and management-training programs provides the basis for this book, which applies principles of business management to the problem of creating greater closeness within the family unit.

REFERENCES

Allport, Gordon W.
  1937   *Personality: A Psychological Interpretation.* New York: Henry Holt & Co.

Argyris, Chris
  1957   *Personality and Organization.* New York: Harper & Row, Publishers.

Argyris, Chris
  1962   *Interpersonal Competence and Organizational Effectiveness.* Homewood, Ill.: Irwin-Dorsey Press.

Berne, Eric
  1964   *Games People Play.* New York: Grove Press.

Bion, W. R.
  1952   Group dynamics: A review. *International Journal Of Psychoanalysis* 33:235–47.

Blake, Robert R., and Jane S. Mouton
  1964   *The Managerial Grid.* Houston: Gulf Publishing Co.

Blum, Richard H., et al.
  1972   *Horatio Alger's Children.* San Francisco: Jossey-Bass, Inc.

Cutler, Beverly R., and William G. Dyer
  1965   Initial adjustment processes in young married couples. *Social Forces* 44, no. 2 (December):195–201.

Dyer, William G.
   1972   Forms of interpersonal feedback. *Training and Development Journal* (July):8–12.

Gibb, Jack R., L. Miller, and G. Platts
   1951   *Dynamics of Participative Groups.* St. Louis: Swift Co.

Harvey, Jerry B.
   1974   The Abilene paradox. *Organization Dynamics* (Summer):63–80.

Herzberg, Frederick
   1966   *Work and the Nature of Man.* Cleveland: World Publishing Co.

Kelman, Herbert C.
   1961   Process of opinion change. *Public Opinion Quarterly* 25 (Spring):57–58.

Luft, Joseph
   1969   *Of Human Interaction.* Palo Alto: National Press Books.

McClelland, David
   1962   Business drive and national achievement. *Harvard Business Review* (July–August):99–112.

Maslow, Abraham
   1943   A theory of human motivation. *Psychology Review* 50:370–96.

INDEX

135

feelings
    accepting, 57–58
    denying, 56–57
    expressing, 17–19, 58–61,
      100–101
freedom of choice, 98–99

Gibb, Jack R., 50
Ginott, Haim, 57
goals, major, how to fulfill,
    109–10

help
    asking for, 91–92
    motives and strategies, 93–96
    offering to, 92–93
    when not to, 95–96
honesty, 74–75

"Increase of love" principle,
    the, 102–3
independence, 37–40
Ingham, Harry, 83–84
interdependence, how to
    achieve, 40–43
interpersonal behavior flow,
    117–18, 120

job enrichment, 33–34
Johari window, the, 83–86,
    87–88

keep-quiet-and-sweat-it-out
    method, the, 12, 13, 121

leveling, 80–81
Luft, Joseph, 83–84

Maslow, Abraham, 111

Milgram, Stanley, 68–69
motivation
    strategies, 31–35
    to change performance,
      29–31

needs, basic human, 111

openness, 42, 79–81, 88

patterns
    changing, 5
    in interpersonal
      relationships, 3–5
priorities, 107–9

reason and emotion, achieving
    balance between, 55–56,
    57–58, 59–60
relationships, authentic, 15–20
rewards and punishment, 31–32
risks, taking, in order to become
    closer, 19–20, 27–28, 90,
    109–10

self-expectations. See
    expectations, self-
sharing, 42–43, 89–90

threat
    coping with, 115–16
    defined, 111–13
    reactions to, 113–15
time, importance of spending,
    with family, 105–10
trust
    bases for, 74–77
    creating, 73–81
    learning how to, 41, 77–81
trust limit, the, 86